THE NORTH WEST COMPANY
Frontier Merchants

This book is dedicated to the frontier merchants and their associates and to the Aboriginal traders, guides and trappers, the voyageurs, the Company Chief Factors, Factors, clerks and servants of yesteryears and the many people in The North West Company family who work today bringing value in foods and services to the people in Northern communities.

Shooting the Rapids by Frances Anne Hopkins
National Archives of Canada, # C-002774

THE NORTH WEST COMPANY
Frontier Merchants

Florida Town

Umbrella Press
TORONTO

Publisher   Ken Pearson
Editor   Olive Koyama
Designer   Judie Shore

Canadian Cataloguing in Publication Data
Town, Florida
The North West Company

Includes bibliographical references and index
ISBN 1-895642-42-6

1. North West Company - History. 2. Hudson's Bay Company - History.
3. North West Company (1967-) - History. 4. Northwest, Canadian, - History.
I. Title

FC3212.3.T68 1998380.1'4397'0971C98-931196-1
F1060.T68 1998

Printed and Bound in Canada

A Three Panes and a Star Publication

Umbrella Press
56 Rivercourt Blvd. Toronto ON. M4J 3A4
Telephone: (416) 696-6665 Fax: (416) 696-9189
E-mail: umbpress@interlog.com

Cover: *Shooting the Rapids* by Frances Anne Hopkins
National Archives of Canada, C-002774
Frances Anne Hopkins was the second wife of Edward Hopkins, Chief Factor of the Montreal Department of the Hudson's Bay Company, which extended from the Mingan District to Fort William. She was able to travel with her husband on his tours of inspection of the trading posts under his responsibility.

She first arrived at Lachine at the age of twenty from England in 1858 as the new wife of Edward and spent the next 12 years in Canada. Her early sketches chronicled her initial period at Lachine and her experiences were captured mainly in pencil, pen and ink, and watercolour. She made at least two trips to Fort William with her husband, the first being in July 1864. In 1869 she and her husband again journeyed to Fort William and returned to Lachine following the old canoe routes in a canoe manned by voyageurs. She was a skilled watercolourist and human activity is often injected into her landscapes as seen with her portrayal of the journeys of the voyageurs. Her husband died in 1893 and she became active in her business of art to earn an income. She died in England on March 5, 1919.

Contents

Foreword

When the new owners of the Hudson's Bay Company's Northern Stores wanted a name for their company, they searched for words that spoke of Canada's heritage, innovation and fair dealing across a vast expanse. The answer seems obvious enough: The North West Company.

Europeans had developed two rival routes to the Canadian West, one through the shallow, ice-bound Hudson Bay almost to the edges of the best fur-producing territories. Since 1662, it had been locked up by an English monopoly. The other, from New France, ran from Montreal, up the Ottawa, along the French River and into the upper Great Lakes. At the head of the lake, the cargoes in the big *canots du maître* were unloaded into the smaller, lighter *canots du nord* for the series of rivers and portages that led into the central plains and beyond. It was the longer, slower route, but the Nor'Westers had to be bold adventurers, moving deeper into the unknown continent, discovering new trading partners and, unconsciously, tracing the economic geography of a country that would someday be called Canada. The *hivernants* or "wintering partners" accepted the hardships and isolation of their lives because they hoped to get rich, and, for many of them, because they fell in love with the land and its people and became the ancestors of European settlement in the West.

In 1760, the French soldiers at Montreal burned their flags and took ship for France. With them went most of the aristocratic and commercial leaders of the colony. At war's end, they believed, the treaty makers would return New France to Bourbon rule and they would regain their lands and businesses. It did not happen. British rule remained, though the Proclamation of 1763 tried to freeze the westward flow of settlement and to preserve the old trading relations between the white and Native peoples of North America. Montreal remained a base for trade with the West, though now English, American and, especially, Scottish merchants and traders managed the warehouses along the St. Lawrence and made the arduous westward journey. In 1775, many Americans rebelled against British rule, in part because Britain had protected Natives and the fur trade. Montreal traders were caught in the middle but their fundamental allegiance was not long in question. The war and the resulting border was a costly disruption: the settlement was a bitter disappointment, but the best of the trade remained north of the line.

In 1779, as the Revolutionary War still raged, a group of Montreal merchants formed their first partnership to carry out the slow, complicated business of buying furs in the West. The partners changed periodically between 1779 and 1821, but the company flag, with its bold "NW", was unchanged from that first year. So was the influence of a tough Scots immigrant named Simon McTavish, who dominated the company from the first, drove its brigades westward, and populated its trading posts and exploring parties with relatives as hard-headed and ambitious as himself. It was the Nor'Westers who moved their depot from Grand Portage in American territory to Kaministiquia and built the great establishment they called Fort William.

It was also the North West Company that inspired Peter Pond, Alexander Mackenzie, Simon Fraser and a score of others whose restless hunt for fresh furs and better routes opened the land and filled our maps with their names. It was Pond who insisted that pemmican was the answer to the Company's need for a light, nourishing food in place of the hunting and fishing that could devour half a day's travelling or more. Of course, anyone who has ever tried the concoction of dried meat, grease and berries may agree that Peter Pond should have had something more than two murders on his conscience.

McTavish's commitment to family loyalties made sense. It could take as long as four years before payment for furs harvested and purchased in the distant Northwest returned from London to the accounts of the wintering partners. That took steady nerves in Montreal and profound trust in the hinterland. The fur business was ruthless and, sometimes, murderously competitive. In addition to the Hudson's Bay Company, with its shorter route and inside track with the British government, there was Jacob Astor's Great American Fur Company, with all the backing a millionaire could buy in Washington, and the rivalry of dissatisfied partners, like Sir Alexander Mackenzie's XY Company.

In the end, the days of competition ended. From 1821, the Hudson's Bay Company set the terms of trade across the vast lands where it held sway. The NW vanished from the Canadian Northwest, and most of its posts fell victim to Sir George Simpson's tireless search for profitable innovation. The Bay ruled from Labrador to Oregon. Its owners drew profits anywhere they could, from whale bones from Fort Chimo (Kuujjuak) for Victorian corsets to the soft coal of Nanaimo for Royal Navy gunboats.

If the North West Company was forgotten, its adventurous spirit remained, pushing trade into the valleys of the Rockies and North to the Yukon and the Arctic barrens. When the Company fully surrendered its monopoly to the newly created Canada in 1868, it shrewdly retained its future as the country's most far-flung land, transportation and merchandising business. It retained a vision, too, of being more than a business, with a responsibility to the people of the Canadian North as well as to its shareholders, and a tradition at least as old as 1790, of adapting to their needs and their expectations.

So an old name for a young company made a lot of sense. The North West Company existed when Native people were sovereign in their own land. It accepted its suppliers and customers as equals, gave and returned fair measure and needed their wisdom and friendship to survive and prosper. The new company may deal in VCRs and personal computers, in freezer chests and potato chips, but who would argue that its human environment is any different?

Desmond Morton
Montreal, Quebec

Hudson's Bay Company Archives / Provincial Archives of Manitoba

Preface

When European adventurers first set foot in North America, they did not find a vacant land. It was inhabited by peoples with different backgrounds and traditions — from the Inuit and Beothuk of the north to the Mayan and Aztec of the south. They were not an homogenous people, they did not share a common tongue, or call themselves by a single name.

Those early arrivals from Europe called the inhabitants Indians, in the mistaken belief that they had arrived on the fabled continent of India, thought to be a land of unimaginable riches. It soon became apparent this was not so, but the name 'Indian' persisted for many generations and was even adopted by the original inhabitants. Many in the United States and Mexico still refer to themselves in that manner. In Canada, 'First Nations people' has become the more sensitive and politically correct nomenclature.

This book traces a history, woven against a background that begins with those early days of contact. For the sake of authenticity in referring to bygone days, 'Indian' has been retained. For correctness in referring to current day events, 'First Nations' or 'First Nations people' has been used. 'Aboriginal' includes both the First Nations and the Inuit people. It is not a perfect solution, but perhaps it will serve to bridge the gap between 'then' and 'now'.

Acknowledgements

One person may write a book such as this, but many others play a role in its creation. For their contribution I am most grateful. To name only a few, Shirlee Smith, of the Hudson's Bay Archives, gave generously of her time and knowledge in reading the original manuscript and making several very sound suggestions. Chris Dafoe and Carol Preston, formerly editors with the *Beaver* magazine, also gave much appreciated critiques. Len Flett, of The North West Company, and others added a Native perspective to the material. Earl Boon, of The North West Company, was an endless source of enthusiasm and encouragement, providing reference material, helping track down information and arranging for me to visit some of the historic sites around James Bay. He also provided introductions to members of The North West family, both active and retired, who gave valuable insights into the "olden days". Rhonda Laxdal's assistance was invaluable.

As my research carried me across the country, I was accorded hospitality and assistance at museums, libraries and historical centres ranging from Fort William to Fort Langley, and from the Peace River to Fort Vancouver. To the staff of each of these facilities, and to the countless others who assisted in varying ways, my gratitude and thanks.

A special thanks to The North West Company who commissioned this work and has provided the financial support to bring this brief history to fruition.

One other contribution must be mentioned. Between 1989 and 1992, a group of students from Lakehead University, under the guidance of Dr. Jim Smithers, co-operating with John Woodworth, of the Alexander Mackenzie Voyageurs Association, re-created the voyages that brought Mackenzie, his Native guides and Métis paddlers from Lachine, Quebec, to Bella Coola, British Columbia, with a side trip to the Arctic Sea. This bicentennial re-enactment followed the original schedule, to the day, along the route. The modern-day voyageurs had many advantages — fibreglass canoes, bug-proof tents and warm sleeping bags. They also had explicit maps and, unlike the original travellers, knew exactly where they were going. Despite this the voyage was, like the original, long, strenuous, dangerous and demanding. It gave interesting insights into the conditions under which Canada's early fur traders worked, and a greater appreciation of the achievement in setting up the supply lines needed to maintain the fur trade.

It was an interesting introduction into the history of both the old and the new North West Company. It literally brought history to life.

Florida Ann Town
Port Coquitlam, British Columbia

Chapter One
Early Trading with the First Nations

He wasn't much to look at. Fat and dumpy, he waddled when he walked and he peered at the world through small, squinty eyes that watered constantly. He had almost no neck. His teeth were stained a deep yellow-orange colour. Timid by nature, he would rather flee than fight, and did much of his work under cover of darkness. All in all, he wasn't very impressive. But he had one memorable trait — he worked hard, and he never gave up. *Castor canadensis*, better known as the Canadian beaver, changed the course of history in North America.

What made him so special? His fur. Beaver fur ranges in colour from a yellowish tan that looks something like a sun-bleached fox, to a deep glossy brown so rich it is almost black. The farther north the beaver lives, the thicker and darker is his pelt. Centuries ago, Europeans fell in love with beaver fur, which was then trapped in England and Europe. At first, beaver was worn only by the nobility. They found the lovely furs beautiful to look at, warm and comfortable to wear, and practical, too. Beaver pelts were waterproof. Soon almost everyone who could afford it wore the beautiful fur. Wealthy tradesmen added fur collars to their jackets and pulled warm fur hats onto their heads. Wives and daughters wrapped themselves in capes made from thick, luxurious pelts and on the coldest days of winter, warmed their hands with beaver muffs. Beaver's popularity continued to grow as people found new ways to make use of it.

It has been estimated that there were as many as ten million beavers in North America before the arrival of the white man. When the demanded for beaver skins for fashion was at its height, there was a danger that the beaver could be eliminated by over-trapping.

BEAVER AND FASHION

In the 1600s, beaver was in demand to make fashionable hats. The supply of beaver in Europe was soon exhausted and interest turned to the North American beaver. Most beaver pelts from North America were destined for the felt-hat industry, initially catering to the fashions of upper society and finally extending to the general public. Styles changed, but the beaver hat continued to be treasured. Demand for this fashion did not end until the late 1880s when the silk hat came into style. Hudson's Bay Company, HBC 58-98/PAM

"Continental"
Cocked Hat
1776

"Navy"
Cocked Hat
1800

Army
1837

Beaver fur is unusual. Unlike most furs, the underfur — that soft, downy hair protected by long guard hairs — has tiny hooks or barbs. Felt makers discovered that these hooked hairs produced a superior grade of felt. Dark and shiny, beaver felt was light, waterproof and sturdy. It was the perfect material for that most important item of male clothing — the hat. Over the years, the shape of men's hats changed. They went from wide-sweeping admiral styled hats to neat, three-cornered hats, from tall top hats to derbies, bowlers and fedoras. Whatever the shape and style of the hat, the very best were made from beaver felt. So close was the association between hats and beavers that at one time, men's hats were simply called "beavers". No man was properly dressed without one.

With the huge demand for pelts, trappers doubled and tripled their harvests. European beavers were soon trapped out. A new supply was needed.

A small traffic in furs had begun among Europeans who fished the Grand Banks near Newfoundland. When they came ashore for a few weeks to dry their catches, they often traded with the local people for a few furs. Sailors and fishermen soon realized these people were no strangers to trading. They knew the worth of their goods, and they expected fair dealing. For years, webs of trading trails had criss-crossed North America, from east to west and from north to south. Everything from silver, salt and sea shells to copper, oils and cedar travelled these trade routes. For the fishing crews, trade was casual at first. They offered whatever surplus goods they happened to have. But the furs they received in trade brought such good prices in Europe they soon made more money from fur than fish.

Beaver was valued by Europeans, but it was honoured and respected by First Nations people. The meat provided tasty meals. Cooked beaver tail was a special treat. Nothing went to waste. Fat was skimmed off and kept for cooking, medicinal and other uses. Teeth and claws decorated ceremonial wear. Even the musk was useful. The beaver used it as a territorial scent marker, but castoreum, a bitter orange-brown substance from the musk gland, made a powerful medicine against headaches. It also reduced fever and eased the aching joints that sometimes affected older people. Modern science has discovered that castoreum contains some of the same ingredients as aspirin, used today to ease headaches, reduce fever and lessen the pain of rheumatism and arthritis.

Clerical
Eighteenth Century

The Wellington
1812

The Paris Beau
1815

The D'Orsay
1820

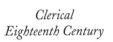

At first European traders were interested only in the fur. Later they also traded for castoreum. Besides its medicinal uses, the perfume industry valued castoreum, using it as a base for its products enabling perfume to retain its fragrance for a long time.

Early adventurers took home more than just beaver pelts. They carried back tall tales about beavers as well, describing beaver lodges as "perfect little buildings" up to three storeys tall, containing numerous rooms complete with windows, balconies and porches. The truth was almost more amazing than the stories. Beavers need water to live. To ensure their water supply, they build dams that reach up to 650 metres in length and more than 5 metres in thickness, creating artificial lakes. In addition they build canals to control the flow of water, gather ground water and seepage, and provide a highway to float their food supplies home. The beaver's reputation for hard work is well deserved. Early fur traders recognized the beaver's reputation when they used it as part of their crests or coats of arms.

Historians don't agree on who first made contact with North America's Aboriginal peoples. The Norse, the Irish and the Portuguese are all believed to have landed on the eastern coast of North America as much as a thousand years ago.

There may have been even earlier contacts. One of the first instances of fur trading in Canada's recorded history took place in Chaleur Bay in 1534, between Jacques Cartier and members of the Micmac Nation. The Micmacs didn't run away when they first saw Cartier's ship, but instead called out and waved furs on sticks to let him know they wanted to trade. They seemed familiar with both Europeans and European trade goods such as knives and iron pots.

During the next century, French and Dutch fur traders arrived in North America and soon became bitter rivals. Algonquians and Hurons took furs down the St. Lawrence River to trade with the French, while Iroquois dealt with the Dutch at Albany, on the Hudson River.

Two adventurers from New France saw the dazzling potential of Canadian furs. In 1659, Médard Chouart, Sieur des Groseilliers, and his brother-in-law Pierre Esprit Radisson, explored the area around the Great Lakes. There Indian traders and trappers shared with them the bounty of furs. The Frenchmen thought their fortunes were made. But the Governor of New France not only refused to give them a licence to trade but also fined them heavily for doing so without his permission.

Seeking redress, Groseilliers and Radisson went to England in 1665 to ask King Charles II for the right to trade in furs using the northern approach through Hudson Bay, also known as the Bay of the North. The king was too concerned with such events as the Great Fire of London and the Great Plague, to consider trading rights in the New World and it was two years before an expedition set out to seek trade.

On June 3, 1668, two ships, the *Nonsuch* and the *Eaglet*, sailed down the River Thames and promptly ran into a storm. The *Eaglet*, badly damaged, limped back to port. However, the *Nonsuch* carried on, reaching the southern end of James Bay on September 29. Expedition members raced to build a shelter before the snow fell. The crude building was called Charles Fort, later known as Rupert's House and Fort Rupert. To the Cree it was, and is, Waskaganish. The next spring, Indians brought furs to the fort to trade, and the *Nonsuch* returned to England with a rich cargo. There was a sudden revival of interest in the proposal of Groseilliers and Radisson and great plans were laid to take advantage of its potential.

Replica of the Nonsuch *under sail in 1972.*
Hudson's Bay Company Archives / Provincial Archives of Manitoba

The Indians knew nothing of these plans, which were based on a totally different concept and system of land holding than they themselves used. The European concept of land holding was not just different, it was totally alien to Indian beliefs and traditions. The Indian people believed that land was made by the Creator for all to use. It did not belong to anyone. They did, however, agree on how to share this gift. Hunting, fishing, trapping and other areas could be assigned to certain families, clans or tribes, to be used for specific purposes. But there was no suggestion that this land was "owned", that others were denied access to it, or that it was held in perpetuity. But there was another, even greater difference.

Charles II shared a European belief that land that was not controlled by a recognized authority was free for the taking. On May 2, 1670, King Charles granted his cousin, Prince Rupert, and 17 others a Royal Charter giving trading rights to the "Governor and Company of Adventurers of England Trading into Hudson's Bay." The area was known as Rupert's Land.

It was quite a gift. Rupert's Land included all land in the watershed flowing into Hudsons Bay, and any other land not directly ruled by "a Christian Prince". In today's terms, the gift included the provinces of Ontario and Quebec north of the Laurentian watershed and west of Labrador, all of Manitoba, most of Saskatchewan, the southern half of Alberta and a large part of the Northwest Territories. In fact, it was almost 40 percent of modern-day Canada and also included territory that is now part of the United States.

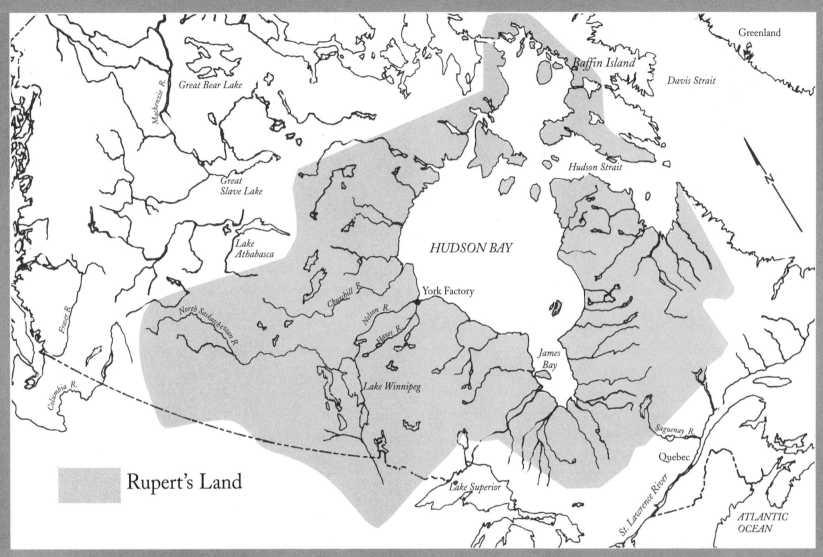

Greenland

Baffin Island

Davis Strait

Great Bear Lake

Mackenzie R.

Hudson Strait

Great
Slave Lake

HUDSON BAY

Lake
Athabasca

Churchill R.

York Factory

Fraser R.

North Saskatchewan R.

Nelson R.

Hayes R.

James
Bay

Columbia R.

Lake Winnipeg

Saguenay R.

Quebec

Rupert's Land

Lake Superior

St. Lawrence River

ATLANTIC
OCEAN

THE HUDSON'S BAY COMPANY

Upon receiving its royal charter, the Hudson's Bay Company quickly established a series of trading posts along Hudson Bay where they could easily receive the annual shipment of food and trade goods sent from England. The HBC strategy was to entice the Native people to collect furs, and then bring them to HBC trading posts.

The HBC could not enforce its monopoly throughout the vast territory it had been granted, but could prevent competitors from using Hudson Bay. Traders from New France responded by moving inland along the waterways of the northern Great Lakes, Lake-of-the-Woods, and lower Saskatchewan River. This international rivalry continued until New France was ceded to Britain in 1763.

Although the HBC began building inland posts during the next twenty years, by the late 1780 a new challenge was being mounted. Scottish traders based in Montreal were venturing beyond the areas controlled by the HBC and, at times, even prevented the HBC from expanding into new territories.

map: Judie Shore

Fur trapping was important in North America long before the first Europeans arrived. Aboriginal peoples discovered where the fur-bearing animals were most plentiful, and developed many methods of trapping and capturing different species. They processed the pelts in a number of ways, depending on how they would be used. Surplus pelts, especially if they were of high quality, could be traded for other valuable objects.

When the Company set up its trading post on the shores of James Bay, it was attempting to break into already established trading routes and partnerships. Indian traders had for centuries traded between Nations. Prime pelts could be exchanged for exotic marine shells from the eastern coast, high quality silica and obsidian from many sources, copper from the Great Lakes area, amber from the North, and prime oils from the far west. Special crafts were highly regarded — intricate quill work and beadwork were valuable, as was jewelry and other decorative materials.

Indians were good trappers and canny traders, and the Company had to choose trade goods that did not duplicate what was already available. Metal objects such as iron pots and knives were popular, as were colourful glass beads and ribbons, cones of sugar and bricks of dried, pressed tea. But the prime objects of desire were the metal traps, guns and ammunition that would make hunting easier.

Business grew quickly, and the Company built three more forts — Moose Factory and Albany Fort (Kashechewan) on James Bay, and Port Nelson (later known as York Fort, still later as York Factory) on the west coast of Hudson Bay.

King Charles's Charter didn't impress the French, who were already settled and trading in the New Land. They attacked British forts by land and by sea. They captured Moose Factory, Waskaganish and Kashechewan, which they called Fort Ste. Anne. Port Nelson was captured and Fort Bourbon established in its place. Later, Bourbon was recaptured by the British and once again became Port Nelson. During the 1680s and 1690s, battles raged back and forth, sometimes leaving only smouldering piles of ashes where a fort once stood, only to be rebuilt in time for the next skirmish.

Finally, in 1697, the Treaty of Ryswick was signed in Europe, bringing France and England to an uneasy peace. The Hudson's Bay Company was almost ruined by then. All that was left was its Albany Fort trading centre. York Factory remained in French hands until 1713, when the Treaty of Utrecht returned "the whole Bay and Straights of Hudson" to England.

During the years of French and British influence in North America, each side formed alliances with Indian Nations. The Micmac and Malecite Nations allied themselves with France, the Iroquois Nations with England.

Under the terms of the 1713 treaty, France was stripped of her possessions on the mainland of Atlantic Canada. Her last stronghold was Louisbourg. By the Treaty of Utrecht, the French retained Cape Breton Island, which they renamed Île Royale, but they did not retain it permanently. Fifty years later, the Treaty of Paris ceded Cape Breton to the British.

While battles raged in Atlantic Canada, the Hudson's Bay Company (HBC) built new forts and tried to increase trade in Hudson and James Bays. Meanwhile, Montreal and American traders became more active. They could not travel through Hudson Bay, but they could and did use the St. Lawrence River and the Great Lakes. From 1713 to 1752 they moved, virtually unchallenged, into some of the richest fur-bearing areas in the known world.

Native traders and trappers watched the rivalry between the various groups and played one against the other to get the best trade goods and the best prices. They knew the value of the resource they controlled.

European traders may have taught the Indian people about guns and ammunition, but the Indians gave an even greater gift: they taught the Europeans how to live in this new land. Snowshoes and toboggans made it possible for the Europeans to travel through the woods in winter. Light-weight canoes opened the rivers and waterways of the country. Indian medicines helped keep the newcomers healthy: some medicines helped cure illnesses and ailments, while others, such as spruce tea, helped prevent them.

As the traders travelled farther inland, they set up alliances with various tribes. Along with the usual trade agreements and business relationships, personal alliances were formed. Many of the traders fell under the spell of the lovely dark-haired, dark-eyed Native women. For some it was a temporary liaison. For others, it was a life-time union.

Family and business alliances helped these traders to increase their fur profits, and siphon away some of the harvest that had once gone to the Company. Critics began to find fault with the Company. It should be more aggressive in its trading. And it was supposed to explore and map the vast territory it controlled. This had not happened.

Cree Indian family, from a drawing by Peter Rindisbacher, who at the age of 15 was among the settlers in the Red River Colony.
National Archives of Canada

The York Factory, the most important larger fort of the Hudson's Bay Company, was located on Hudson Bay.

Hudson's Bay Company Archives / Provincial Archives of Manitoba

One of the harshest critics was Arthur Dobbs, who prepared a report for the King on conditions in the "Countries adjoining to Hudson's Bay, in the North-West Part of America." Dobbs harped on the Company's failure to find a passage to the Western Ocean, or to even look for it. Worse, he said, it discouraged others from the search. Again and again, like the chorus of a popular song, he repeated his claims that the Company did nothing to encourage exploration and further trade, only sat and waited for the Indians.

The Montreal traders were definitely not content to wait for trade. They actively sought it, roaming farther and farther afield, establishing ties with the people of the First Nations. Their business boomed and trade routes lengthened.

Finally the company stirred, but only slightly. In 1743, in a cautious experiment, they opened Henley House, a tiny post at the junction of the Albany and Kenogami rivers. The idea of expansion was not popular. In 1749, James Isham, Governor of York Factory, told a British committee that inland posts would serve no useful purpose and argued against leaving the Bay area.

About this time, a new group of players entered the game. In 1746, in the Highlands of Scotland, a furious battle finally had ended — the Battle of Culloden. It was a cruel and vicious defeat for the Scots. Many heart-sick survivors looked for a new way of life, in a new land. Opportunity called in North America. It was an easy decision for many. Hundreds of young, tough, self-reliant Scots left their villages and crofts eager to throw themselves into a new way of life in a new land.

The Scots made an easy alliance with French, Indian and Métis traders and trappers. They liked and respected these people. Moreover, they enjoyed the freedom and independence of this new way of life. The tribal system may have reminded them of ties within their own clans. Soon the Scots were sending word home, urging family and friends to join them in North America.

Meanwhile, the fury that raged between Britain and France erupted once again. The Seven Years War officially began in 1756, although it had been rumbling along unofficially before then. Seven bitter, bloody years after the war was declared, it ended, on February 10, 1763, with the signing of the Treaty of Paris. Under the terms of the Treaty, the French government withdrew from Quebec.

French-Canadian traders shrugged their shoulders and continued to do what they had always done. They made new alliances and built new business. They made serious inroads into HBC profits, and diverted trade from HBC forts.

In 1763, York Factory traded more than 30,000 made beaver — beaver pelts that were stretched and cured. During 1768, they handled only 18,000. These figures opened even the blindest eyes. The head office in London sent Matthew Cocking and Samuel Hearne to open Cumberland House, about 100 km west of The Pas, Manitoba, at Pine Island Lake, on the Saskatchewan River.

As trading forts went, this was relatively close to home — only 750 km from Fort York and less than a third of the distance the Montreal traders had to travel, using the much longer route along the St. Lawrence and Great Lakes waterway. To paraphrase a later expedition, it was a small step for Hearne and Cocking, but a giant step for the Company.

Chapter Two

Montreal Traders Form a Partnership

Once again, war disrupted the lives of the Indian people. During the American Revolutionary War, the Mohawk Nation allied itself with the British. They were joined by the Cayuga, Seneca, and Onondaga. When the British were defeated, their Indian allies could not return to their homes in the victorious thirteen states.

The British did not abandon their allies. As a reward for their loyalty, Britain gave land on the north side of Lake Ontario, at the Bay of Quinte, to one group of Mohawks. Another, larger group received land along the Grand River, about 80 km south of the modern city of Kitchener, near Brantford. Nearly 2,000 Indian Loyalists settled in Brantford, mostly Mohawk, Cayuga and Onondaga, along with some Seneca, Oneida, Tuscarora, and a few others who had also lost their traditional lands.

The largest of the land grants included all land to a depth of 10 km on each side of Ontario's Grand River, from mouth to source.

Joseph Brant, one of the Indian leaders, believed the land was an outright gift to be used in the best interests of the people. Hunting could not support the large number of immigrants, and traditional farming methods did not produce enough food to meet their needs. Brant sold or leased some parcels of land to raise money so they could switch to the more productive European style of agriculture. The government was outraged. They said the land could not be sold or traded without their approval. The Indians saw this as government interference and continued to sell and lease their land to raise much-needed funds. The squabble continued until 1841, when the Crown reclaimed what was left of the land and set it up as an Indian reserve, but by this time only a small part of the original grant remained.

Opposite: **The fur trade could not have existed without the aid of Canada's Native people. They trapped and skinned the animals, and prepared the pelts for trade. They also provided the traders with food and taught them travel skills — canoes, snowshoes and toboggans were all Native inventions. As the traders moved farther from their own settlements, Natives acted as guides and interpreters.**

Glenbow Archives

The large number of people moving into the area displaced those who were already there. They had to go elsewhere, displacing other groups in a ripple effect that created widespread disruption. Some members of displaced Nations joined fur traders who were extending their territories to the west. Most were Catholic Mohawks from the Caughnawaga, Oka and St. Regis districts. They were valued trappers, traders and voyageurs, and established a place for themselves. But the Micmac and Malecite Nations, former French allies, fell on hard times. English settlers, including many British Empire Loyalists who fled the United States after the War of Independence, moved into Atlantic Canada. The Micmacs and Malecites were crowded from their traditional hunting and fishing grounds. Too many trappers worked in too small a space.

All too soon, beaver and other valuable animals were trapped out and game stocks were depleted. The Algonquians, Nipissings and Iroquoians spread to the north and west, searching for new sources of fur. They pressed into areas previously controlled by the Cree Nation, forcing the Cree to move as well.

About this time, England took over the fur traffic which had been controlled by the French. Indian trappers and traders were joined by free traders based in Montreal. These free traders were a mixed group, and came from many places: French Canada, America, Scotland, Ireland, Germany, Holland.

There were many reasons to become a free trader. Some enjoyed the lifestyle. Some wanted to escape from problems at home. Some looked for excitement. Some dreamed of finding riches. And some held secret dreams of finding the North West Passage. The man who discovered that fabled route to China would be rich beyond imagining. The early French traders even named one of their settlements La Chine (China), a name it bears to this day in the more familiar form of Lachine. Almost every trader had a story to tell about the Passage, and the Western Sea beyond the Shining Mountains. They were convinced it was tantalizingly close at hand.

As the free traders plunged farther and farther into the wilderness, it became more and more difficult to operate independently. The greater distances and the short length of time between thaw and freeze-up made it almost impossible for one man to buy, sell and transport furs in the same season. Small groups of free traders combined, forming partnerships that changed from year to year.

During the 1770s, the newest route to riches was along the Saskatchewan River. The area was filled with independent traders. At the mouth of one of the Saskatchewan's tributaries, the Sturgeon River near modern-day Prince Albert, seven different groups vied for trade. Many of the free traders put up with incredible hardships. Some staved off starvation by chewing bark, pelts and scraps of leather. Frostbite left its agonizing marks on fingers and toes. Scurvy attacked the teeth. But the traders hung on, grimly.

In 1778, Peter Pond was one of a small group of traders who found themselves with a surplus of trade goods at the end of the season. Pond decided to winter over. He was eager to find new sources of pelts.

When his partners returned to Montreal, taking their pelts to market, they passed the Height of Land, between Lake Superior and the Lake of the Woods. Each voyageur may have taken a moment to remember his first crossing, and the traditional ceremony that was part of that event.

That fall Pond had no time for distractions. He was racing against the onset of winter and every day — indeed, every hour — counted. With four canoes carrying the remainder of their trade goods, Pond's group followed their Indian guides to a place that was supposed to be rich in beaver. The guides led them up the Churchill River to Methye Portage, where they dragged their goods and canoes to the top of an 800-metre ridge. On the other side they saw the Clearwater, flowing towards the Athabasca River. Even today it is an awesome sight, but the voyageurs may have been too weary to appreciate it.

Given more time, and different conditions, Pond may have recognized this passage, but the savage breath of winter was nipping at his ears. His party pressed on 60 km south of Lake Athabaska, and built a crude cabin. From there they began trade with the Chipewyan. The furs were even better than Pond's guides had promised. In the springtime, he returned with 140 packs of superb pelts. He left behind an equal number because he had no way to carry them.

North West Company coat of arms
Hudson's Bay Company Archives /
Provincial Archives of Manitoba

HEIGHT OF LAND

When a wintering partner reached the Height of Land flowing into Hudson Bay for the first time, ice cold water from a nearby stream was sprinkled on him with a cedar bough. Then he repeated the voyageur's vow: he would never permit a newcomer to cross the Height of Land without making him a Nor'Wester, and he would never kiss another voyageur's wife without her permission. A toast in high wines and the firing of a gun completed the ritual.

Pond's Indian guides and companions had taught him how to live off the land. He carried strips of dried meat and wild rice and augmented this with fresh foods — fish, meat, and greens from the woods — whenever he could. Pond travelled fast and he travelled light.

When Chipewyan trappers offered him some pemmican he was quick to try it — and to appreciate the value of this new food. Light, durable, and highly nourishing, it was the key to travel in this country. Pemmican was made from dried buffalo, elk or deer meat pounded into a powder, mixed with dried berries, poured into a leather bag, then sealed with grease. The bags were easy to store in a canoe. Pemmican gave Pond the most valuable gift of all — time. Small amounts of pemmican replaced large amounts of meat and fish. Paddlers could spend time on the river, instead of hunting or fishing. They could travel greater distances before the freeze-up stopped them.

Original seal of the North West Company, with its strong motto of "Perseverance". The beaver below the tree not only showed its significance but also was a symbol of the industry of the company.

Courtesy of Old Fort William

As Pond's furs began their long journey to Lachine and the warehouse at Montreal, serious discussions were underway there. Britain had placed an embargo on private shipping on the Great Lakes to ensure that no guns, goods or ammunition reached American rebels in the Thirteen Colonies. Respecting that embargo, the governor of Quebec had decided not to issue licences to the fur traders. The traders argued and pleaded with him, but by the time he relented it was too late for trade goods to reach the Athabasca. And it was far too late for the provisions needed in 1779-80 by the *hivernants,* traders who spent their winters out in the field.

The merchants were desperate. Some were ruined and returned to Scotland, but others remained. Most agreed their only hope was to band together. If the governor would not listen to small, independent traders, surely he would listen to a coalition of traders in one big partnership. It was the beginning of the North West Company.

The strategy worked. The 1780 licences were issued on time. One of the traders, Simon McTavish, realized that even small partnerships could not maintain the long supply routes that now stretched to the North West. By pooling their resources, a group of traders might be strong enough to survive both the wilderness and the competition.

When the North West Company (NWC) was formed, it went through five distinct stages. The first NWC co-partnership formed in Montreal in 1779 was followed by the partnerships of 1780-82; 1783-87; 1787-1804, and the partnership of 1804-21. The North West Company propelled Canada through four decades of turmoil, excitement and expansion. When it was over, the country would never be the same again.

The Montreal coalition of 1779 controlled the fur trade along the St. Lawrence. It included the firms of Isaac Todd & McGill, Benjamin and Joseph Frobisher, McGill & Patterson, McTavish & Co., Holmes & Grant, Wadden & Co., Ross & Co., Oakes and Co. and McBeath and Co. McBeath's was the company that employed Peter Pond, whose Athabasca fur discoveries were about to revitalize the trade.

The North West Company's roster changed over the years, but the 1779 group did contribute one lasting mark: a company flag. The distinctive, "NW" banner flew for the first time in 1779.

Among the partnerships, McTavish & Co. is worth special notice. It was headed by Simon McTavish, a Scots immigrant who entered the fur trade as an apprentice at the age of 13, sorting furs in a stuffy New York warehouse. Before too long, he established himself in Montreal, started his own company and took in Patrick Small as a partner. Small was the great-nephew of a governor of Guernsey, and the nephew of Britain's famous General Small.

Patrick Small was the wintering partner in the firm, spending his time at Île à la Crosse. There, his young Native wife brought him the entire trade of her tribe. The young couple had two little girls, Charlotte and Nancy. Soon after her fourteenth birthday, Charlotte was to marry another well known North West partner, David Thompson.

McTavish's rise was meteoric. Only eight years after becoming a partner of the North West Company, he became a senior partner. His actions influenced the entire fur trade and he was the driving force behind many innovative programs. One of his major concerns was attempting to wrest power away from the Hudson's Bay Company. He was one of many who tried to negotiate transit rights for the North West Company through Hudson Bay to reduce the ever-increasing distances the NWC canoes were forced to travel. He never succeeded. In fairness, neither did anyone else.

At one point, he backed a group of British subjects who claimed Charlton Island, near the mouth of the Rupert River in James Bay, for the North West Company. His nephew, Angus Shaw, was one of the group who took physical possession of the site.

Shaw and John George McTavish, Simon McTavish's cousin, used Charlton Island as a base to build two new posts, one at the mouth of Moose River and the other at the mouth of East Main River. Both were soon abandoned, but today The North West Company operates stores near those locations: Moose Factory and Eastmain.

McTavish and his relatives permeated the fur trade. As the company grew, so did the list of McTavish's relatives. In addition to John George McTavish and Angus Shaw, the trade included John McDonald of Garth, who married one of McTavish's nieces; Roderick McKenzie, who married McTavish's sister-in-law; Simon Fraser and John Fraser, both cousins; his great-nephews Simon and Joseph McGillivray; Alexander Fraser, a distant cousin; Judge Reid, who married yet another of McTavish's nieces; James McTavish, a relative of unknown closeness; and Donald McTavish, another cousin. There were also uncounted numbers of clansmen for whom McTavish found jobs in the trade.

Simon McTavish (1750–1804)
Hudson's Bay Company Archives / Provincial Archives of Manitoba

"The names of the North West Company's partners sound like a roll-call of the clans of Culloden. These men were hardy, courageous, shrewd and proud. They spent a good part of their lives travelling incredible distances in birchbark canoes, shooting rapids, or navigating inland seas. They were wrecked and drowned. They suffered hunger and starvation. They were robbed and murdered yet they built a commercial empire the like of which North America at least has never seen."

Dr. W. Stewart Wallace

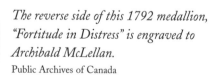

Beaver Club Jewels
Gold medallions were awarded to new members of the Beaver Club. The NWC motto, "Industry and Perseverance", appears on this side.

THE BEAVER CLUB

A social club, founded in 1785 in Montreal, it was limited to those who had spent a winter in *le pays d'en haut*, and been initiated as voyageurs. In addition, candidates for membership had to be accepted by unanimous vote.

The meetings of the Club were boisterous. Banquets were held bi-monthly during the winter when fur traders were settled in Montreal. Along with traditional rites, there were five obligatory toasts: to the Mother of all the Saints; the King; the fur trade; the voyageurs, their wives and children; and absent members. This was followed by much drinking and a good deal of bragging.

The rules of the Beaver Club required every member to attend every meeting. The only allowable excuse was poor health. At the meetings, members re-staged *le grand voyage*, sitting on the floor, using whatever came to hand as imaginary paddles. Stroking furiously, they sang the songs of the voyageurs. Their imaginary canoes soon faced imaginary rapids and they had to clamber across the tables and chairs as they paddled on to their imaginary destinations.

Today, the Club still exists and once a year members gather for a dinner party in the Queen Elizabeth Hotel in Montreal. Membership continues to belong to an exclusive group of people, but, of course, the qualification that a member must have spent a winter in *le pays d'en haut* no longer is a requirement.

McTavish was a generous man. In addition to finding jobs for numerous relatives, he paid for the education of his sister Ann's son, Simon, and his brother's two sons, William and Duncan.

Early in the autumn of 1787 Montreal entertained its first Royal visitor, Prince William Henry. One of the highlights of the Royal visit was a glittering formal ball at the Château de Ramezay. Simon McTavish was presented to the Prince as a respected member of Montreal's business community. It was a far cry from his early days in the fur trade. And as a handsome, financially secure bachelor, he was a welcome addition to Montreal's busy social scene. At dinner he enjoyed fine wine, good food, and the company of pretty women who laughed at his jokes and blushed at his compliments.

In 1785, a group of North West Company partners had formed the Beaver Club. Membership was restricted to the 55 partners who had been initiated as wintering partners — that is, they had wintered for at least one season beyond the Height of Land west of Fort William. McTavish had never wintered beyond Fort William, but in 1795, in recognition of his role in the formation and success of the North West Company the Club made him an honorary member.

The reverse side of this 1792 medallion, "Fortitude in Distress" is engraved to Archibald McLellan.
Public Archives of Canada

Curiously, for all McTavish's love of family and his intense devotion to those who claimed family allegiance, he was still a bachelor well into his forties. That changed abruptly when he fell head over heels in love with Marie-Marguerite Chaboillez, one of the seven daughters of his old friend, Charles Jean Baptiste Chaboillez. McTavish enjoyed only eleven years of marriage before he developed a serious illness and died, in 1804. He was 54 years old.

During the long winters in Montreal, "in-town" partners often met to discuss common problems. The harsh conditions in the field, government interference, new areas of exploration and other concerns fuelled their talks.

Each spring when the canoes set out from Lachine, carrying trade goods and provisions, they followed the same route — past the Long Sault Rapids on the St. Lawrence, portaging the Rideau and Chaudière Rapids on the Ottawa River, across Lake Nipissing, then down the French River into Georgian Bay. There they paused. Indian and Métis paddlers made a traditional offering of tobacco to the Creator who controlled the winds. Soon each traveller joined in, making gifts of tobacco or small trinkets as they asked for a safe voyage

The traders must have longed for as simple a solution to another vexing problem: the actions of politicians and statesmen in far-off countries, whose decisions so greatly influenced their lives.

Everyone knew that England had to give independence to the British colonies on the Atlantic seaboard. The colonists had fought long and hard for the right to be free of British rule. Now all that remained to be settled were the terms of that freedom.

THE QUEBEC ACT

The Quebec Act of 1774 provided for the extension of the Province of Quebec to the Ohio River. By this Act, commercial opportunities were opened for fur traders and others in Quebec. Later following the American War of Independence, the Treaty of Versailles, changed the borders. Under this Treaty, the newly independent United States of America was extended across the Alleghenies to the Mississippi River, curtailing opportunities for the Montreal fur traders.

Fur traders in Montreal and Quebec were stunned when the Treaty of Versailles, signed in 1783, spelled out those terms. The Quebec Act had set the boundary of Canada along the Ohio River. The Versailles treaty set a new boundary between the infant Republic and Canada, slashing across territory that was of key importance to fur traders. The new boundary line followed the Pigeon River west from Lake Superior, then along the 49th parallel to the headwaters of the Mississippi. The Mississippi did not reach the 49th parallel, but no one was to discover that until several years later. Gone were the trading posts at Niagara, Detroit and Michilimackinac. Gone was free use of the Grand Portage. That famous route, near the head of Lake Superior, was well south of the new border. The British government banned the direct export of furs from Canada to the United States. The valuable American market could now be reached only by shipping furs from Montreal to London, then back across the Atlantic to New York. The added transportation costs left Canadian furs at a terrible disadvantage in the American market.

The company moved its headquarters 60 kilometres northeast to the mouth of the Kaministikwia River, on Lake Superior, where they constructed a trans-shipment centre with 42 buildings set in a rectangle, on a 50-hectare site near the river. They built their own workshops, with a cooperage for making kegs and a boatyard to build and repair the special canoes used by North West crews. The new location was called Fort William, after William McGillivray.

The North West Company could no longer use the Grand Portage to ship furs to American markets, but traders continued to use the trail to transport goods from one Canadian centre to another. The Americans, however, couldn't ignore the tide of furs and trade goods passing through their area. Before long they issued a series of orders and restrictions that made portaging increasingly difficult. Soon they threatened to impose heavy duties on the trans-shipped furs as well.

There were more problems ahead. The logistics of transporting goods for the wintering partners, and supplies for both the paddlers and the partners, became all but impossible. Somehow, the North West Company had to find a way to provision their canoes and trading posts without hauling food all the way from Montreal. Peter Pond remembered the pemmican his Indian guides had shared with him. It was the perfect solution and became increasingly popular with traders. It provided variety to the traditional quart of ground corn and dab of grease that formed the daily ration for *hivernants* and traders, and was a high-energy food for the hard-working crews of the canoe brigade. Suddenly the demand for pemmican escalated.

First Nations entrepreneurs saw a new avenue of opportunity. Assiniboine and Western Cree largely abandoned their traditional role as middlemen in the fur trade and become provisioners to the trade. They drew on vast herds of prairie buffalo as a source of dried meat, grease and pemmican.

By 1795 the Hudson's Bay Company, North West Company and independent traders had more than 21 posts operating along the Assiniboine River. Soon the supply business proved more profitable for the Assiniboine and Western Cree than the fur trade had ever been.

York boat, seen here on Split Lake, northern Manitoba, 1928.
Hudson's Bay Company Archives / Provincial Archives of Manitoba

Canoes had always been important to the fur traders. As lines of transport lengthened, they became crucial. The North West Company was able to compete with HBC traders largely because of the speed and flexibility of their canoes. HBC traders were accustomed to the York boats, high-sided wooden boats which were rowed, not paddled, and whose crews had to stand to row. While the York boat was ideal for transport around Lake Winnipeg and Hayes River, the Company directors didn't seem to understand the difference between travelling on lakes and on rivers. They instructed their crews to use the larger boats to carry larger loads. Voyageurs hooted with laughter as they watched HBC men build and row the clumsy, heavy craft on the Saskatchewan River.

Nor'Westers relied on two types of canoes: Montreal canoes, or *canot du maître*, large freight canoes with ten paddlers, which handled up to four tonnes of freight, and the smaller *canot du nord*, with six paddlers, which carried about two tonnes of trade goods and pelts, all carefully wrapped into standard bundles of about 40 kg for portaging. The small canoe was light enough for two men to carry across the portages. This was important, as there were many portages on each of the canoe routes.

PORTAGES

There were 36 portages between Lachine and Georgian Bay. They were called *décharges* when the voyageurs had to carry both canoe and cargo. If they could lift the canoe through a portage and had to carry only the cargo, it was called *décharge*. *Posés* were resting places established by the voyageurs. A grand portage consisted of 16 *posés*.

CANOES

As fur companies expanded their network of posts, they developed extensive supply routes, which were served by waterways.

Birchbark canoes were the vessel of choice. They were light-weight, built with a bark covering over a spruce frame. Spruce resin was used to seal the seams. Although they appeared fragile, they were amazingly strong. If repairs were needed, they could be effected easily with materials available from the bush, such as sheets of bark, resin, and spruce roots.

Large freight canoes and York boats were used on the major rivers and lakes. Further inland, goods were carried in smaller canoes. Rapids and heights of land between rivers meant that canoes and freight had to be portaged.

This was hard work. Men could carry up to three packs at once, each weighing 40 kg., across the portage. Several such trips may have been needed to pack everything across one portage.

The canot de maître, *which could carry up to 4 tonnes, was used mainly on the journey from Montreal to Fort William. The smaller* canot du nord *was used mainly on smaller lakes and rivers west of Lake Superior.*

above: Provincial Archives of Manitoba

Large freight canoes brought the North West Company's goods from Lachine to its major distribution and supply centre at Fort William. There, goods were transferred to the smaller northern canoes that made it possible for NWC traders to reach their far-flung posts before freeze-up. In the autumn, the process was reversed. Voyageurs paddled the small canoes, each with its precious cargo of furs, to Fort William, where loads were combined in the larger Montreal canoes and taken to Lachine.

As the bulk of the trapping and trading passed west of Rainy Lake and Lake of the Woods, many Indian bands in that region left the fur trade to become canoe makers. It was a satisfying use of their traditional skills, and paid enough that they could still enjoy the tea, sugar and European goods which were now part of their daily lives.

With so many far-flung forts and depots, it was hard for the Lachine partners to know exactly where their traders were. In many cases, traders and trappers were not quite sure if they were even on the right side of the recently established boundaries between the United States and Canada. Russia and Spain had also established colonies in North America, but no one knew exactly where their territories began or ended. The question of accurate maps became more important than ever.

PADDLE STROKES

A good voyageur averaged 50 strokes per minute, all day long. The pace was slightly faster when travelling upstream, against the current. Voyageurs' paddles were slimmer and shorter than most modern paddles, but the steersman's paddle was longer to help him manoeuvre the boat.

Chapter Three
The Nor'Westers

In 1788 a young trader joined the North West Company. His name was Alexander Mackenzie. He was to take provisions to Peter Pond at Lake Athabaska, and winter there. Unfamiliar with the territory, Mackenzie left too late. Freeze-up stopped him at Lac La Loche (the Methye Portage). Canoes were useless in winter so he unloaded them and separated his goods. Essential provisions went on a sled, the rest were cached, or hidden. Mackenzie followed his Indian guides on foot, while his crew dragged along toboggan-loads of goods. Lake Athabaska was very short on supplies that winter.

Mackenzie's introduction to the area was a series of visits to Athabaskan subposts, stretching as far north as the Great Slave Lake and southwest to the Peace River. His cousin, Roderick McKenzie, was stationed nearby, wintering with Patrick Small, Simon McTavish's partner.

The long, northern winter nights passed quickly as Peter Pond told his new apprentice stories about trading and trapping. Alexander Mackenzie listened avidly. He could not have had a better teacher. Pond knew his area well. But he knew more than that. He had talked with Indians who travelled the Peace River, and told him of the "Great River" and "Shining Sea" beyond the mountains. Pond was convinced that the river (the Columbia), discovered by Captain Cook, and the Pacific Ocean were only a little way beyond Lake Athabaska, and he presented his case to anyone who would listen.

Pond was something of an enigma: at one moment he seemed everything a northern trader should be. He could live under difficult conditions, he inspired tremendous loyalty among his staff, and he was a thoughtful and intelligent man. He respected the Indian trappers and traders, and they returned that respect. Some reports say he was illiterate, but as he prepared maps and handled the business of a trading post, this seems unlikely.

Opposite: **At age 29 Alexander Mackenzie of the North West Company could claim the honour of being the first European to cross North America, north of Mexico, by land. Today, his red pigment and bear grease message is recreated in cement on a rock in Dean Channel, near Bella Coola, British Columbia.**

Painting by Jim McKenzie, commissioned by The North West Company

But Pond either had a black side or was dogged by misfortune. The winter before Mackenzie's arrival was a bad one. Pond had made two successful trips to Athabaska but, caught by an early freeze-up on the third trip, had to winter at Lac La Ronge. Etienne Wadden, a former Nor'Wester now operating as an independent trader, was already there, but Pond was determined to trade at La Ronge too.

During the winter, tempers flared. There were no witnesses to the event, but one of Wadden's clerks said Wadden was killed while Pond was visiting his cabin. Pond was charged with murder.

A few years later, Pond was involved in another slaying. John Ross had been a North West Company partner but was not part of the company's 1784 agreement. Ross joined a smaller outfit

Detail from illustration by C.W. Jefferys.
Public Archives of Canada #C73431

which competed with both the HBC and the North West Company. Ross and Pond had a series of arguments during the winter. Finally, a dispute over some fish nets led to a scuffle and Ross was killed. Pond and his men were charged with Ross's death. The charges were later dropped for lack of evidence, but Pond was heartsick over the whole event. In 1787 he sold his share in the North West Company to William McGillivray (McTavish's nephew) for £800 and left the fur trade.

Throughout his years as a trader, Pond was frustrated by the need to spend so much time carrying out business. He dreamed of exploring the vast empty reaches of the Athabaska and the country beyond.

Mackenzie was determined he would not be locked behind the counter of a trading post. Like Pond, he hoped to find a route to the Pacific. First, he would need a reliable clerk to look after things while he was gone. Who better than his cousin Roderick? Roderick agreed, and returned to the northwest for a seventh season instead of taking a long-awaited vacation. While Mackenzie set out for Pond's old post, gathering and pressing furs, Roderick took charge of building Fort Chipewyan, the company's new post on Lake Athabaska.

Right: This is a fascinating map that shows a perception of what the northern part of the continent looked like, at least to this map maker. It might have led to the common misconception of how close the west coast was to the middle of the continent.
The author's collection.

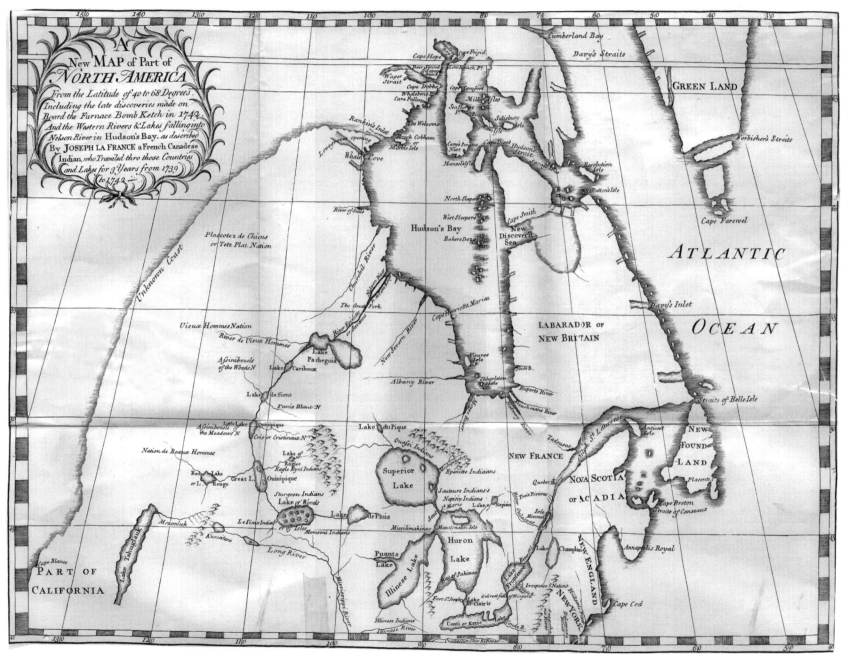

A New MAP of Part of NORTH AMERICA From the Latitude of 40 to 68 Degrees. Including the late discoveries made on Board the Furnace Bomb Ketch in 1742. And the Western Rivers & Lakes falling into Nelson River in Hudson's Bay. as described By JOSEPH LA FRANCE a French Canadese Indian, who Travelled thro those Countries and Lakes for 3 Years from 1739 to 1742.

TRADING VALUE

Trading with the Native Peoples was by barter. The value of the trading goods was expressed in furs in terms of a whole beaver or "made beaver" (M.B.), the pelt of a perfect, full-grown beaver which had been properly cured and weighed about half a kilogram.

M.B.	TRADE GOOD
1	$3/4$ lbs of coloured beads
1	1 $1/2$ lbs of gun-powder
1	1 brass kettle
1	2 lbs of sugar
1	1 gal. brandy
1	2 yds flannel
1	12 doz. buttons
1	1 pair breeches
1	1 pair shoes
1	20 flints
1	8 knives
4	1 pistol
11	1 gun (varied with length)
1	2 pair looking glasses
1	2 hatchets
1	20 fish hooks
1	1 blanket
1	2 shirts

In the summer of 1788, while Roderick took their furs to Grand Portage, Mackenzie set out in search of the Northwest Passage.

He followed the Slave River into Great Slave Lake, past the junction of the North Nahanni and the Great Bear River. As he paddled, his dreams evaporated. The river ran in the wrong direction. Five weeks later he reached the tidewaters of the Beaufort Sea and the Arctic Ocean. Mackenzie had travelled and charted the great river that now carries his name, but he had not found the Northwest Passage. The trip back to Fort Chipewyan was a gruelling race against freeze-up, made even worse by disappointment. The next summer, Roderick was left to manage the fort while Alexander Mackenzie returned east. There he learned that a Hudson's Bay Company surveyor, Phillip Turnor, had located the position of Fort Chipewyan. Not only was it far north of the 49th parallel of latitude, it was 10 degrees farther east than Mackenzie and Pond had believed. Mackenzie realized that if he knew more about surveying and map making, he would be better prepared for the challenges that faced him.

The North West Company was growing at such a rate that the senior partners had to reorganize the business. McTavish and Frobisher were now responsible for storing, preparing, shipping and selling furs. In addition, they handled all the company accounts and acted as bankers for surplus funds. John Gregory and Daniel Sutherland looked after all business at Grand Portage, leaving Simon McTavish free to spend more time in London.

Beaver tokens made of brass were first issued by the Hudson's Bay Company in 1884 as a medium of exchange. This token had a value of 1 "made beaver". It shows the Company monogram and the initials of the district, EM (East Main). Notice that the engraver made a mistake and inscribed "NB" instead of "MB" for "made beaver." On the other side is the Company coat of arms. The standard medium of exchange in the fur trade, "made beaver" (MB), which was a beaver pelt of an adult male in prime condition. Hudson's Bay Company Archives / Provincial Archives of Manitoba

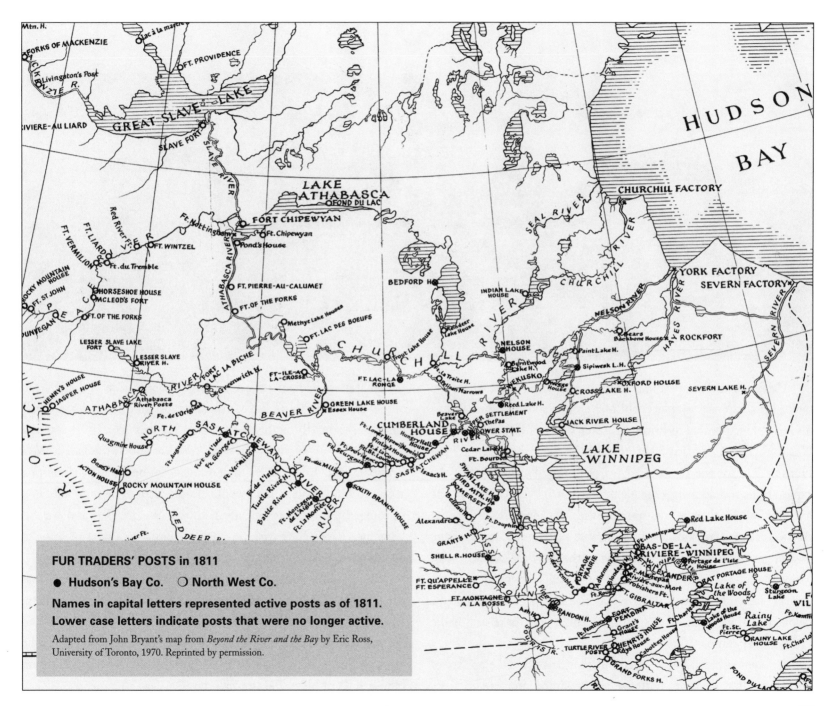

FUR TRADERS' POSTS in 1811

● Hudson's Bay Co.   ○ North West Co.

**Names in capital letters represented active posts as of 1811.
Lower case letters indicate posts that were no longer active.**

Adapted from John Bryant's map from *Beyond the River and the Bay* by Eric Ross,
University of Toronto, 1970. Reprinted by permission.

HUDSON BAY

GREAT SLAVE LAKE

LAKE ATHABASCA

CHURCHILL FACTORY

YORK FACTORY
SEVERN FACTORY

LAKE WINNIPEG

FORT CHIPEWYAN

CUMBERLAND HOUSE

HBC's Post, Fort Chipewyan on Lake Athabasca, north of Edmonton.
Hudson's Bay Company Archives / Provincial Archives of Manitoba

McTavish had many things to look after in London, where the major fur auctions took place, but one project above all was dear to his heart. He appealed to Prime Minister William Pitt to cancel the Hudson's Bay Company charter, with its exclusive right to use Hudson Bay for the fur trade. McTavish proudly told Pitt of the explorations and discoveries made by the North West Company. He told Pitt of Mackenzie's voyage, up the Mackenzie River, to the Arctic Ocean. This journey, he said, was just one example of the many trips of exploration undertaken by the North West Company, which had no special privileges whatsoever. Under the circumstances, he said, it was only fair that the Bay's charter should be revoked so the North West Company could also make use of the Hudson Bay route.

Pitt sympathized but pointed out that it would take an Act of Parliament to cancel the charter, a lengthy procedure.

McTavish had no time for that. His next stop was the head offices of the Hudson's Bay Company, with an offer to lease transportation rights through Hudson Bay. He was refused. It was not the first attempt, and it would not be the last one. If the North West Company couldn't shorten their transportation lines by obtaining access to Hudson Bay, they would simply have to be more efficient in using the route they already had, the Great Lakes and the St. Lawrence River. McTavish set about assembling a fleet of ships to do just that.

Back in the field, the wintering partners were ensuring that McTavish would have lots of furs to move. In 1790 Peter Pangman, a partner in the North West Company, made the farthest move to the west yet recorded. Following the North Saskatchewan River, he came within a few kilometres of present-day Rocky Mountain House and cut his initials into a pine tree.

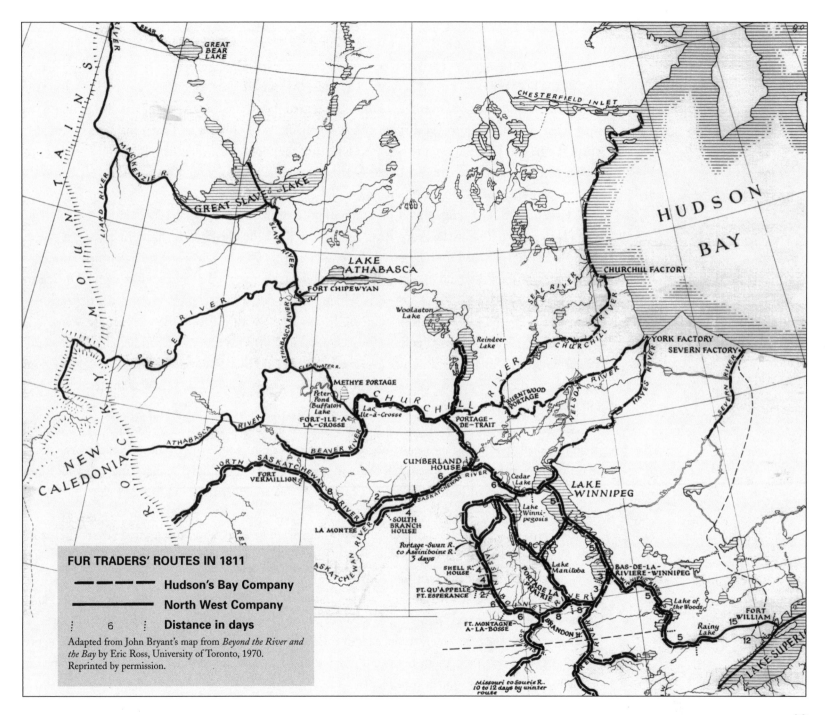

FUR TRADERS' ROUTES IN 1811

– – – – – – Hudson's Bay Company

————— North West Company

⋮ 6 ⋮ Distance in days

Adapted from John Bryant's map from *Beyond the River and the Bay* by Eric Ross, University of Toronto, 1970. Reprinted by permission.

Sir Alexander Mackenzie
Hudson's Bay Company Archives /
Provincial Archives of Manitoba

Meanwhile, unknown to McTavish, Alexander Mackenzie had followed him back to England. Mackenzie was so disturbed over the results of his trip to the Arctic Ocean that he decided to take a year away from the fur trade to learn more about surveying, mathematics and map making. It would be worth the time if he could acquire both the skills and the tools that would help him find a route to the Pacific Ocean across uncharted country. During this time, the faithful Roderick was left behind to spend yet another year at Fort Chipewyan.

Mackenzie worked diligently at his studies and returned to the Athabaska country the following year. He decided to follow the Peace River on his search for the Pacific. Somehow, he managed to convince Roderick to stay at Fort Chipewyan for one more year. Mackenzie wintered in a little log shack at the junction of the Peace and Smoky rivers, so he could set off as soon as spring thaw came. During the winter he gathered six canoe loads of pelts, which he sent down to Roderick. He added a personal note to his cousin: "I send you a couple of guineas, the rest I take with me to traffic with the Russians...."

In May 9, 1793, Mackenzie and his Indian guides set out. This time, they paddled upstream against the current, to the Great Divide. Once over the height of land they followed streams flowing west, coming at last to the river that would one day be called the Fraser. Mackenzie followed this river for about 650 km through endless portages.

His guides told him the river soon turned south. Mackenzie believed he was on the Columbia, but when he calculated the distance from where he was to the point where the Columbia reached the ocean, he realized it was farther than he could travel in a season. He did not have enough time or enough supplies. Another group of Native people told him there was an alternate route to the ocean — overland, along a trading trail that led due west.

Mackenzie cached his canoes and followed the Eulachon Trail, a traditional trade route that led to Bella Coola and the Pacific Ocean. The journey lasted 17 days, covering about 400 km through lush undergrowth, before reaching the Coast.

When he arrived he was met by hostile Indians brandishing weapons. Just one month earlier Captain George Vancouver's ship *Chatham* had explored these very waters. One of Vancouver's men had fired a gun at the Indians, which accounted for the angry reception given to Mackenzie. Mackenzie presented gifts and reassured them he would not fire at them. But he realized he was not welcome and decided to head back as soon as possible.

Before leaving, Mackenzie mixed a little vermilion colouring with melted grease and wrote on the face of a large rock in the Dean Channel, *Alexander Mackenzie, from Canada, by land, the twenty-second of July, one thousand seven hundred and ninety-three.*

Mackenzie had reached the tidewaters of the Pacific Ocean. He was the first European to record an overland crossing north of Mexico, but he had not discovered a route for the fur trade. Nor had he met either the Russians or the Spaniards, though both had settlements on the Pacific.

Mackenzie and his men hiked back to the river, then clawed their way upstream to the Great Divide. After long days of struggle and hardship, the downstream run was almost pleasant. They passed their wintering post at the junction of the Peace and the Smoky rivers and soon arrived back at Fort Chipewyan. Their journey had taken 134 days.

The next summer, Mackenzie travelled to Grand Portage to see Simon McTavish, but McTavish was still in London. His nephew, William McGillivray, replaced him at the annual meeting.

During the winter Mackenzie had had a good deal of time to think about the fur trade and to ponder on the competition between his company and the Hudson's Bay Company. It seemed a dreadful waste of time and money. There were enough furs for all.

But that was the least of it. Competition between the two companies had led to fights and resulted in needless deaths. Without the fierce competition between traders, the fatal incident between Peter Pond and Etienne Wadden might never have happened. There were many other such incidents, he knew.

Mackenzie and McGillivray travelled together after the meeting at Grand Portage. At Niagara-on-the-Lake they called on the Lieutenant-Governor of Upper Canada, John Simcoe. Mackenzie told Simcoe about his voyage to the Pacific, then shared his thoughts on the fur trade. The North West Company and the Hudson's Bay Company should unite, he said, and share the Hudson Bay route. They could build fur depots on the Pacific Ocean, to avoid the long, expensive overland route. A unified company could share Pacific Coast depots with the East India Company, to everyone's mutual benefit.

Simcoe listened carefully to Mackenzie's comments and passed them along to London, but no action was taken.

Mackenzie returned to the field to face more pressing problems. The winterers at Grand Portage had serious complaints against the company. Conditions in the field were harsh and they wanted a larger share of the profits. Their trade goods were not always as good as those offered by the Hudson's Bay Company, and that made trading difficult. McTavish was so often in London that they felt no one was listening to them.

The wintering partners turned to Mackenzie with their complaints because they felt that he, at least, would understand the hardships they suffered. Mackenzie did what he could to help. It wasn't much, but it earned the men's gratitude.

Mackenzie was the man of the moment, but other stars were rising in the North West Company firmament. One of the brightest was David Thompson.

Thompson was raised in the Grey Coat School in Westminster. He was 14 years old when he became a Hudson's Bay Company apprentice. Thompson trained under Samuel Hearne and Humphrey Marten, and dreamed of becoming an explorer. Later, he studied surveying. About this time he began what became a life-long habit of recording information. Weather records, plant and animal life, local customs and languages and many other things were carefully written into his journal.

During the winter of 1796, when he was still with the Hudson's Bay Company, Thompson was posted to Reindeer Lake. Here he met Alexander Fraser, one of Simon McTavish's numerous relatives. The two young men got along well and were friendly competitors. Thompson's contract was coming up for renewal.

After 13 years with the Bay, his annual salary was £60, and he could get bonuses. Generous enough, but not as tempting as Fraser's prospects with the North West Company. As a partner, Fraser's returns were larger and his opportunities were greater. That spring, Thompson decided to join the North West Company.

He was warmly greeted when he arrived at Grand Portage in the summer of 1797. The Nor'Westers urgently needed a man with his skills. A new treaty, the Jay Treaty, allowed Canadians to transport goods across land that was now American territory, but a number of their trading posts were now on American land. They needed to know exactly where the border was before they built new posts. Most of all they needed a Canadian connector between Lake Superior and Lake Winnipeg.

During the next year, Thompson travelled the North West Company routes, visiting trading forts and depots, searching out the headwaters of the rivers and scouting out the international boundary. He returned to Grand Portage the following summer with charts showing the exact location of every post in the area and its relationship to the international border. Thompson's next assignment was to the Athabaska country, where he combined surveying and exploring with some very profitable trading.

GREY COAT SCHOOL

The Grey Coat School in Westminster, England, was an institute that was "designed to educate poor children in piety and virtue". Thompson has been described as a 'fatherless boy', as he was an orphan when his father died when he was only two years old.

FORT WILLIAM

Located on the northwest shore of Lake Superior, Fort William was the main centre for the North West Company and together they formed a colourful chapter in Canada's history. As the Nor'Westers moved deeper into the interior regions of Canada in search of furs, it became increasingly difficult for the voyageur canoe brigades to penetrate the western interior, pick up the furs and return to Montreal before the winter freeze up. A transshipment point midway was needed. At first, they used Grand Portage, near Pidgeon Lake. However, in 1783 the border with the United States was established and the ensuing threat of customs duties forced the Nor'Westers to find another base and they re-established the old French route of the Kaministiquia River. In 1803, they held their Great Rendezvous at Fort Kaministiquia. In 1807, the name was changed to Fort William, named after William McGillivray, who was Chief Director of the NWC from 1804 to 1821.

Fort William became the main hub in the Nor'Wester's network. Besides serving as the warehousing depot for trade goods, provisions and furs and the transshipment centre, it became the site for the annual meeting of the Company's Directors and Partners. It was the fur trade post for the trade of the local Native peoples and the quarters for the lodging, provisioning and equipping of the NWC personnel. Fort William was essential for the success of the Nor'Westers.

With the merger of the North West Company and the Hudson's Bay Company in 1821, Fort William declined in importance. It became little more than a fishing depot and over time the buildings began to deteriorate until the Fort was closed in 1831.

Left: Aerial photo shows the restructured Fort William open to the public in 1973 to portray its colourful past. Courtesy of Old Fort William

Below: A view of Fort William from a watercolour by Robert Irvine.
Hudson's Bay Company Archives / Provincial Archives of Manitoba

43

Meanwhile, there were several important changes within the Company. McTavish continued to deal generously with his relatives and with clan members back in Scotland. When his partner, Joseph Frobisher, died in 1796, McTavish appointed his nephew, William McGillivray, as his new partner. Not only was William promoted to a senior partnership, but his brother Duncan was also brought into the firm.

Around this time, Alexander Mackenzie and McTavish had a falling out, possibly because Mackenzie realized that with the never-ending supply of McTavish relatives, his chances for promotion in the firm were being eroded. Matters came to a head in the summer of 1799, at Grand Portage, during a meeting between him and William McGillivray.

There are no records left to tell the story, but when the meeting was over, Mackenzie quit the North West Company. He returned to London and worked with a ghost writer to complete his famous book, *Voyages from Montreal, on the River St. Lawrence through the continent of North America, to the frozen and Pacific Oceans; in the years 1789 and 1793, with a preliminary account of the rise, progress and present state of the fur trade of that country.*

The book was an instant success. Mackenzie found himself famous, and he revelled in it. In 1802 he received the greatest honour he could have hoped for: King George III made him a knight of the realm.

Sir Alexander Mackenzie then returned to Montreal where he was met by a new group of partners. John Forsyth and his cousin, John Richardson, of the highly respected firm of Forsyth & Richardson, joined forces with John Ogilvy, of Parker, Gerrard and Ogilvy, along with John Mure of Quebec, to become the New North West Company, known as the XY Company. The XY mark distinguished the New North West Company from the North West Company. Mackenzie was one of the senior members of the firm, which was now in direct competition with both the Hudson's Bay Company and his former associates in the North West Company. In 1803 the new company was reorganized under the official name of "Sir Alexander Mackenzie and Co." but it continued to be known as the XY Company.

The XY mark was soon seen all across the northwest. When the Company ordered a new boat, especially designed for use on Lake Superior, they named it *Perseverance*. It was a name that had long been associated with the North West Company and was, in fact, part of the company's crest. Mackenzie's cheek in thus naming his boat must have infuriated his former partners. XY posts sprang up at Rainy Lake, Bas de la Rivière Winnipic, and on the Red River. An XY fort appeared on the Assiniboine and new posts were built in the Qu'Appelle valley.

Simon McTavish met the new challenge with all the thunder and fury that had carried him against challengers in the past. He told clerks to undersell the XY Company in every way possible, to increase rations of rum and tobacco, and to win Indian trade with more and better gifts. Once again, competition escalated into violence. The setting was at Fort de l'Isle, on the Saskatchewan, where the North West Company, the XY Company and the Hudson's Bay Company all had trading posts.

James King was a North West employee who had formerly worked for the XY Company. An XY employee named LaMothe learned that King was coming to trade at a nearby village. LaMothe planned to visit the same band, so the two men travelled together and camped together overnight, near the band's village. In the morning, King discovered some of his packs were missing. He accused LaMothe of taking them and an argument broke out. Suddenly a shot rang out, and King lay dead in the snow.

A grieving LaMothe carried the body by sled back to Fort de l'Isle, where King was buried with military honours. LaMothe was tried and acquitted. Not all confrontations between rival traders ended in death or injury, but acts of violence were becoming more and more common. Finally the government acted to bring some form of law and order to the Northwest. In 1803, five Justices of the Peace were appointed. They were William and Duncan McGillivray, Sir Alexander Mackenzie, Roderick McKenzie and John Ogilvy.

XY COMPANY

The XY Company was the name popularly used for the New North West Company formed in 1798 by Forsyth, Richardson and Company of Montreal and Leith Jamieson and Company. It was in opposition to the North West Company. It was said that the name originated in the designation "XY" while the goods of the North West Company were labelled "NW" to avoid confusion.

In 1803 the XY Company was reorganized by Alexander Mackenzie under the name of Sir Alexander Mackenzie and Company. In 1804 it was absorbed in the North West Company.

NATIVE WOMEN IN THE FUR TRADE

Native women, played an essential role. Those who married the newcomers taught them the language and customs of the country, as well as providing them with the clothing and equipment essential for survival in western Canada and in the North. The wives prepared traditional foods by picking berries, catching fish and capturing small game, all of which they dried for later use. Berries and dried meat, mixed together with fat, made pemmican, the nutritious food that became the mainstay of the fur trade. The women were also skilled in the use of plants and herbs to heal injuries and prevent disease.

THE RENDEZVOUS

Rendezvous was one of the highlights of the voyageur's year. In late August or early September, traders tallied accounts and readied the season's harvest of pelts for travel. One partner would winter over, the other would speed back to Fort William.

At the Rendezvous, traders turned in their furs, selected trade goods for the next year, exchanged news and information with each other, then celebrated the end of the season. As many of the Montreal partners as possible would attend the Rendezvous. For many it brought back memories of their own years as traders.

After spring breakup, traders headed back to their wintering partners (called *hivernants*) with fresh trade goods, provisions, and as much of the news as they could remember.

1803 was a landmark year in many ways. New Fort, on Lake Superior, replaced Grand Portage. New Fort was on the old and almost forgotten French route. Originally called Fort Kaministikwia, the old French fort had been established in 1717, abandoned by 1759 and eventually destroyed by fire. Roderick McKenzie learned of it from a group of Indian guides and reclaimed the site for the North West Company. Construction soon began and before long the new fort at the mouth of the Kaministikwia River was open. At last there was an all-Canadian route and the problem of transporting freight across American lands had been solved.

During the first Rendezvous at New Fort, in 1804, David Thompson became a partner in the North West Company. Four years later, when the 42 buildings within the fort were complete, its name was changed to Fort William in honour of Senior Partner William Simon McGillivray. It was the pride of the North West Company.

The XY Company was quartered in much smaller buildings, in the Little Forks area across the river During this same period, there was troubling news from the United States. The young Republic had purchased the Louisiana Territory. Now it needed to know just how large that territory was, and exactly where it lay.

The government sent Captain Meriwether Lewis and William Clark to map the territory and to search for an overland route across the continent. Canadian traders waited anxiously for word of the Lewis and Clark expedition, worried lest the Americans lay claim to either the fur trade of the Upper Missouri River or the vast, rich territory west of the Rockies.

In 1805, a young North West Company partner, yet another relative of Simon McTavish, followed Indian guides on another voyage of discovery. His name was Simon Fraser and, like Alexander Mackenzie, he searched for the river that would serve as a trade route to the Pacific Ocean. Fraser followed Mackenzie's route, up the Peace River, then along the Parsnip River, building trading posts along the way. When he reached Nakazleh (Fort St. James) he built another outpost.

The open valleys and spectacular mountains in the area reminded him of the stories his mother used to tell him about her native Scotland. In her honour, he called the district New Caledonia (New Scotland).

Fraser left Fort St. James, crossed the wind-whipped waters of Stuart Lake, paddled down the Nechako River, still following Mackenzie's route, to the Williams Lake area. Here Mackenzie had turned aside, taking the overland route to the ocean.

Fraser carried on, believing he was now on the Columbia River. The trip was a nightmare. He had never imagined such drastic and dangerous conditions as those he found in the rapids and canyons of this river. When he reached its mouth, he realized he was too far north to be on the Columbia. His river did reach tidal waters, but it was too wild and dangerous for commercial use. Sadly, he traced his way back through the narrow canyons and turbulent waters of the Fraser River.

Fraser may have been disappointed, but his journey was not a complete loss. Like Mackenzie, he had charted the area and established a British presence in previously unmapped territory.

The North West Company had sent two expeditions in search of the Pacific Ocean. Both had reached their goal, but neither route was usable. The secret of how to get to the coast by way of the Columbia River remained a mystery.

Simon Fraser in the Fraser Canyon on his journey to the sea, 1808.
John Innes, Native Sons of British Columbia and Simon Fraser University

Chapter Four
A Merger Born of Violence

On July 6, 1804, at the age of 54, Simon McTavish died. He did not live to see the fulfilment of his dream — a union of fur traders joining the North West Company, Hudson's Bay Company, and XY Company. His nephew, William McGillivray, named in McTavish's will as the new head of the company, decided to make that dream come true.

He began, on November 5, by bringing together two of the three rivals — the North West Company and the XY Company.

The two companies had many trading posts in close proximity to each other, once the basis of sharp competition, but now merely duplications. To cut costs, many were closed. Canoe loads were standardized. Pelts were pressed into tight bales, weighing about 40 kg, and wherever possible all other goods, such as sacks of flour, were packed in the same sized loads. Wintering partners and their clerks had always been allowed treats for their own use. Now these perks were cut in half. Partners could have only a little over 2 kg of tea, less than 2 kg of coffee and the same of chocolate for the entire year. Clerks received half that amount. Voyageurs were allowed no treats but could bring out, freight free, either two buffalo robes or two dressed skins on their return trip to Montreal.

The combined trade of the two companies produced a flood of furs. Once again, transportation became a critical problem. The long supply lines cost far too much in time, money and manpower. Once again the partners approached the Hudson's Bay Company, requesting permission to use the Hudson Bay water route. Once again they were refused.

Opposite: David Thompson at Surprise Rapids on the Columbia River.
Painting commissioned by The North West Company.

MONTREAL TRADERS

The Montreal fur trading companies were dependent upon the Native people of western Canada. They needed guides to lead them into new trading areas, and translators to help them understand the languages and cultures. The Native people were, themselves, active traders, and had been so for generations. Without their knowledge of the trading trails which crisscrossed the continent, it would have been impossible for Montreal traders to find their way across the country or to establish trade.

Sir Alexander Mackenzie tried a different strategy. He went to London, prepared to purchase stock in the Hudson's Bay Company. As shareholders, the North West Company would have a vote on the actions of the company. At the same time, Mackenzie applied to the British Board of Trade for a charter allowing the North West Company to trade in the Far East, where the East India Company held a charter similar to the charter granted the Hudson's Bay Company.

There was more involved than simple trade. The North West Company had very real concerns about the actions of John Jacob Astor, a German immigrant who lived in New York. Over the past 20 years he had built two large companies, the Great American Fur Company and the Pacific Fur Company. He was determined to take American trade to the shores of the Pacific Ocean.

Allowing Astor to go unchecked would give the Americans a strong claim to the Upper Missouri country. The Nor'Westers were still smarting over the earlier loss of territory, especially the loss of the Grand Portage. They didn't want history to repeat itself.

A share in the East India and South Seas trade would allow them to maintain a small post at the mouth of the Columbia River. A small naval force could also occupy the post. It would protect the country against American claims and give protection against Spain, who still held posts along the California coast, and buffer Russian claims as well.

Mackenzie waited three years while the Board of Trade leisurely debated the question. In the meantime, Astor offered the North West Company a one-third interest in the American Fur Company. The offer was refused.

At this point, McGillivray came to a separate agreement with Astor and formed the South West Company, to recoup some of the business that was being lost. The North West Company partners were uneasy about some parts of the agreement, but were eventually persuaded it would be to their best advantage.

North West Company half-penny token, about 1820.
Bank of Canada Museum

Through all this period, the Board of Trade continued its slow deliberations in London. Meanwhile, David Thompson set out on the Company's third major venture to discover the Columbia River. Mackenzie had failed, Fraser had failed, but Thompson was determined to succeed.

David Thompson was unique among the Nor'Westers. Many spoke one or two Indian languages, but Thompson learned four — Chipewyan, Mandan, Piegan and Kootenai — and compiled rough dictionaries in each of these languages.

In 1806, following Indian guides and accompanied by his wife and family, Thompson worked his way across the Great Divide. In the Kootenai country, he floated his supplies up the river to Lake Windermere, located in an open valley along the shoulder of the Rocky Mountains. Here he built Kootenai (Kootenay) House, using it both as a trading centre and his own headquarters for exploration.

Over the next few years he built further outposts: Kullyspell (Kalispell) House, on Lake Pend Oreille, and Saleesh House, at Thompson's Prairie in present-day Montana. Now he was ready to begin a survey of the entire Columbia River. He made his way to the Chinook salmon fishery at Ilthkoyape (today known as Kettle Falls) and set off down the river.

The Columbia is a bewildering waterway. It loops and doubles back on itself and rivers flow into it from every point of the compass. Along one stretch, the Kootenay runs parallel to the Columbia but in the opposite direction. Further downstream, the two join. Today, controlled by locks and dams, the Columbia seems serene and placid, but this powerful river drops a total of 805 metres between its source and the sea, and in its natural state it was formidable.

*A*t the junction of the Snake and the Columbia, Thompson posted a paper claiming the territory for Great Britain and the North West Company. Then he continued his journey along the river, passing the landmarks known today as The Dalles, Mount Hood and the mouth of the Willamette River. On July 15, 1811, David Thompson reached the Pacific Ocean.

Astor had beaten him. The Pacific Fur Company's ship *Tonquin* had arrived on April 11 and established Fort Astoria, a collection of four log huts in charge of two former North West Company clerks, McDougall and Stuart.

VOYAGEURS

Voyageur was the term applied to canoemen of the inland fur trade. Generally, voyageurs were French Canadian or Métis, although some were Native persons and a few were Scots. They reached the height of their fame under the North West Company.

The voyageurs were surprisingly small in stature, but very strong and able to paddle long distances in the course of a day. Typically, their day began at first light (around 3 o'clock in the morning) and they paddled until about 8 a.m. before stopping for breakfast. Then they continued paddling until noon, when they would pause for a brief lunch. Throughout the day there would be short breaks called 'pipes' — each just long enough to stoke up a pipe of tobacco — then they paddled until around 9 p.m., when their day ended with supper cooked on the shore.

Thompson made his way back up to Kootenai House and the following year journeyed back to the annual Rendezvous in Fort William. There were eager questions about the new route and the posts he had established. Then talk turned to other, more urgent matters. Tension between the United States of America and Great Britain was growing. The implications were serious.

On June 18, 1812, the United States of America declared war on Great Britain. The North West Company's posts were in many cases on the front line of battle. Detroit was captured by the British, then abandoned. A group of North West Company volunteers, under William McKay, recaptured Fort Prairie du Chien on the Mississippi. McKay's volunteers were one of three NWC regiments, each between 800 and 1000 men, who formed the Corps of Canadian Voyagers.

THE *NANCY*

The *Nancy,* which had transported the bulk of the company's goods between Georgian Bay and Ste Marie, was sunk by the Americans at the mouth of the Nottawasaga River in August, 1814. All that remains of the *Nancy* is the burned hull, which is on display in a special museum dedicated to the *Nancy* at Wasaga Beach on the Nottawasaga River.

Even as the battle raged, fur trading continued. Fort Niagara was no longer safe to use, so the North West voyageurs travelled by way of York, on Lake Ontario, using Yonge Street as a portage to Lake Simcoe. Armed American vessels, the *Tigress* and *Scorpion*, patrolled Lake Huron. In 1814, the NWC ship *Nancy*, transporting goods between Georgian Bay and Ste. Marie, was sunk by the Americans at the mouth of the Nottawasaga River. Then the Americans scored another victory at Put-In-Bay, on Lake Erie.

The North West Company felt trapped. Once again they appealed for permission to use Hudson Bay. Permission was granted — at a cost of £10,000 per year. The price was too steep. The Nor'Westers decided to take their chances and continue to use the Ottawa River. Luck was with them and there were no serious incidents.

While the United States and Great Britain fought in the East, conflict escalated on another front, between the North West Company and Astor's Pacific Fur Company. It was like a rerun of the old North West and XY Company battles.

Happily, no lives were lost.

British blockades prevented the passage of supply ships from eastern seaports, depriving the Pacific Fur Company of desperately needed stores. The North West Company supplies continued to arrive by overland routes. Early in 1813, one of Simon McTavish's numerous relatives, John George McTavish, and John Stuart, set out for the mouth of the Columbia. On arrival, they negotiated with Duncan McDougall to purchase Fort Astoria. In October, McDougall agreed to the sale. There was a condition: McDougall and some of his staff would be readmitted to the North West Company as partners. The Pacific Fur Company flag was struck, the North West Company flag run up, and the post renamed Fort George.

A company clerk named Angus Bethune witnessed the bill of sale. The following year, Bethune would set out for China, to establish the North West Company in that country. It was the first of two NWC ventures to China. Neither was successful — costs were heavy, profits were small and there were many problems. Still, during this period, the North West Company controlled the Pacific Slopes, firmly established from San Francisco to the Alaska border.

The NWC sites were shown on a huge map that hung in the mess hall at Fort William. David Thompson's masterpiece, *The North West Territory of the Province of Canada*, accurately displayed the span of the Company's empire. The North West Company forts, along with competing Hudson's Bay Company forts, gave weight to Britain's claims to a broad band of North America, territory that stretched across the continent from sea to sea.

Lord Selkirk, 1771–1820
Hudson's Bay Company Archives / Provincial Archives of Manitoba

Soon, however, another European treaty, the Treaty of Ghent, struck a blow to NWC plans. All territories seized by force during the war were to be restored. The Americans claimed Fort Astoria had not been sold, but captured as an act of war. Britain gave up its place at the mouth of the Columbia River. The Nor'Westers were aghast, but an even darker cloud loomed on the Company's horizon, generated by a young man who was born Thomas Douglas, at Kirkcudbrightshire, in Scotland.

Thomas was the youngest of seven sons born to the Earl of Selkirk. He had no hope of assuming the title, but within a few years each of his six brothers died. He became the fifth Earl. After graduating with a law degree from the University of Edinburgh, he visited France and saw the results of the revolution that had recently overturned society in that country.

Thoughtfully, he compared the plight of the French with that of his own countrymen, and the desperate conditions in the Scottish Highlands. Thousands of small crofters (farmers) had been driven from their rented farms by English landlords, who made more profit from sheep. In many cases the crofters and their families were literally starving.

When Selkirk read Mackenzie's *Voyages* in 1802, he was inspired. There were vast stretches of good land in the interior of Canada. The climate seemed gentler than on the North Sea and the shores of the Atlantic. It seemed to Selkirk that here, Scottish crofters could be "...certain of comfortable subsistence & they may raise some valuable objects of exportation...."

53

Below: **Fort Gibraltar was a trading
post of the NWC on the bank of
the Red River, near its junction
with the Assiniboine River. It was
built about 1809 and demolished
shortly after the arrival of the
Selkirk settlers. Fort Garry was
built on its site in 1821-22.**

He suggested a resettlement project to the British Government, but they turned him down. Selkirk didn't give up. He set up his own plan to move 800 displaced crofters to Prince Edward Island. His motives were of the best, but his good deed was short-circuited by his lack of preparation. No food or shelter was available for the settlers. A few years later, he repeated his resettlement project, this time moving crofters to land grants at Moulton, on Lake Erie, and at Baldoon, on Lake St. Clair.

Once again, neither site was suitable and there was neither food nor shelter for the settlers. After struggling against overwhelming hardships, the immigrants left Selkirk's lands as soon as they could.

Still, he continued with his schemes and dreams. Now Selkirk turned to the Hudson's Bay Company. He already held stock in his own name. In 1807 he married Jean Wedderburn, who also held a block of Hudson's Bay Company stock. When he approached the Hudson's Bay Company directors with his latest scheme, it was not as an outsider but as an important shareholder. The directors listened to his plan to move Scottish crofters to the Red River Valley, to a place he called the Selkirk Settlement. By this time the Nor'Westers had managed to buy a few shares of HBC stock. When Selkirk's proposal was brought up at a shareholders' meeting, they protested violently. It didn't make any difference. The Bay gave Selkirk some 18 million hectares of land, straddling the Red River, to house a minimum of 1,000 families. It was an area almost three times as large as Scotland itself.

RED RIVER SETTLEMENT

The Red River Settlement was founded on the banks of the Red River by Lord Selkirk in 1811. Selkirk's wife, Jean Wedderburn, was a major stockholder in the Hudson's Bay Company and her brother, Andrew Colvile, later became Governor. Selkirk obtained 27,454,000 hectares (106,000 square miles) from the company and sent a party of Scottish and Irish colonists to establish a colony at Red River. The first group, consisting of about 100 colonists, reached their destination in 1812.

The North West Company challenged the title of the HBC to Rupert's Land. They feared that the colony would be a threat to the supply of pemmican.
A further attempt to establish a colony in the Red River area was thwarted by the affair at Seven Oaks in 1816. In 1817, Selkirk re-established the colony when he came from Montreal with a support force of experienced army veterans recruited from army regiments.

Hudson's Bay Company Archives / Provincial Archives of Manitoba

FUR TRADE CEREMONIES

Trade between Native peoples had always been more than just an economic activity. It was a chance to establish relationships between individuals, families, and nations. When trading partners met, they renewed their relationships by sharing the pipe and exchanging gifts. These were important parts of the ceremony.

When fur-trading companies entered the trading arena, their Native guides introduced them to the trading ceremonies, which were such an essential part of the transaction. Just as each group of fur traders had leaders, so, too, did the Native groups. Individuals designated as Trading Chiefs would meet with the Chief Traders from the fur traders, share the pipe and other gifts. The Trading Chief usually offered prime beaver pelts while the Chief Trader would give muskets, blankets, rum and foods such as raisins, sugar or tea.

The land grant included parts of present-day North Dakota, Minnesota, Manitoba and Saskatchewan. It also included a number of North West Company pemmican trading posts, including Esperance and Dauphin on the Qu'Appelle; La Souris; Gibraltar, at the junction of the Red and Assiniboine rivers; Pembina; and Bas de la Rivière Winnipic. The North West Company was furious, but the Métis were frantic. The Métis were a distinct society, drawn from unions between the early French traders and their Indian wives. Their settlements were mostly in the area of the Red River. Now they were threatened by the dream of a man from a distant land.

The saga of the Selkirk Settlement is one of the sorriest in Canadian history. Immigrants came to Canada under appalling conditions. When they arrived, nothing was ready for them. They travelled late in the year and were totally unprepared for the harsh winter conditions they encountered They had not time to build adequate shelters, or to lay in supplies. Starvation, scurvy and exposure killed them. The few who survived to the springtime still could not improve their situation. They had no ploughs to break the land or plant their crops.

The North West Company, for all its protests against the Settlement, helped those early settlers to survive. Soon a second wave of settlers poured in to the area. Things might still have been worked out, but yet another group of immigrants arrived, all lacking the basic necessities. Once again, nothing was ready for them and food was in short supply.

Alexander Macdonell was a Nor'Wester, in charge of the company's Red River department. By a quirk of fate, the man Lord Selkirk hired as his agent to set up the Selkirk Settlement was Miles Macdonell, Alexander's cousin.

Miles herded his clutch of settlers from one site to another, trying to get them established. By 1814, they were beginning to build homes and work the land.

Miles Macdonell marked the occasion by sending an official proclamation to his cousin at Fort Gibraltar, stating ".. no persons trading in furs or provisions for the Hudson's Bay Company, the North West Company, or individual traders, will be allowed to take out any provisions — meat, grain or vegetables — from the Selkirk territory...." A few exceptions were listed, but to claim them the traders needed a licence from Macdonell. He signed the proclamation "Miles Macdonell, governor of Assiniboia."

Many Métis made their living by hunting buffalo and making pemmican to sell to both HBC and NWC traders. Macdonell did not spare them. They were forbidden to run buffalo on horseback, their traditional method of hunting, or to sell pemmican to the North West Company.

The Métis ignored Macdonell's order.

Miles brought the matter to a head soon after when his men seized a load of pemmican from a group of Métis, tried to seize another load being rafted down the Assiniboine to Fort Gibraltar, then took 400 bags of pemmican from La Souris. He placed cannon in front of Fort Douglas. In October, Macdonell told managers at Fort Gibraltar, Bas de la Rivière Winnipic and Fort Dauphin they, and everyone in their posts, had six months to leave. The land no longer belonged to the North West Company. It was now Lord Selkirk's property.

It was war between the Selkirk Settlement and the North West Company. It was common knowledge among the Nor'Westers that many of Selkirk's settlers would leave if they only could. The settlers had had enough of hunger, deprivation and danger. And most had had enough of Miles Macdonell.

Duncan Cameron, acting for the North West Company, applied for a warrant and arrested Macdonell and his sheriff, a man named Spencer. Then Cameron offered transportation to all of Selkirk's settlers who wanted to leave Assiniboia and journey to Canada, or to farm land near other settlements. Some settled near Bradford. Most others left for Lake Winnipeg. Once the settlers were out of the way, Fort Douglas was burned to the ground.

Unhappily, the action settled nothing. Colin Robertson, a former Nor'Wester who now worked for the Hudson's Bay Company and was also Selkirk's agent, stepped into the battle. He gathered the colonists together again, rebuilt Fort Douglas, and resettled them there.

THE SLAYING OF OWEN KEVENY

Owen Keveny was born in Sligo, in northwestern Ireland. He left in June, 1812, as one of Lord Selkirk's second party of settlers, bound for the Red River colony.

Keveny landed at York Factory in August of that year and finally arrived at the Red River Settlement in October. In 1813, he returned to York Factory where he was employed by the Hudson's Bay Company for the summer, after which he returned to Europe.

He returned to Canada to be an accountant for the HBC and spent the winter of 1815-16 near Moose Factory. In the summer of 1816 he was in charge of a party of men sent to restore order to the Red River Settlement. He was a hard disciplinarian and several of his men deserted. When he arrived at Bas de la Rivière, he was arrested by a group of Nor'Westers. He was never brought to trial, but was killed while under arrest.

Charles de Reinhard confessed to being involved in Keveny's murder, was tried at Quebec and sentenced to death. The sentence, however, was never carried out. There were questions about the jurisdiction of Lower Canada courts over an event which took place in Indian Country. As a result, de Reinhard was released from custody.

Robertson rightly saw that the settlement would never succeed unless he loosened the close ties between the Métis and the North West Company. He began paying sky-high prices for everything he bought from the Métis, gave out presents of blankets and trade goods, and hired Métis to hunt for the colony.

While Robertson was busy undermining the North West Company, another group of settlers arrived in charge of Robert Semple, who announced that he was now the governor-in-chief of Rupert's Land.

Meanwhile, the business of the fur traders went on. In the fall, Cameron, NWC's manager at Fort Gibraltar, left for his usual tour of the outlying posts. When he returned he wrote his reports for Fort William. Along with the usual items of business, he asked for help in solving the problem of the Selkirk Settlement. His request came a little too late.

Robertson's men took Cameron prisoner and seized Fort Gibraltar, then captured Pembina. Robertson left for England, taking his prisoner with him and leaving Semple in charge. Semple's first act was to demolish Fort Gibraltar. The flames that burned Gibraltar lit a fire in the hearts of the already smouldering Métis. They saw the deed as clear evidence of what lay ahead for them.

Cuthbert Grant, a 19-year-old leader of the Métis forces, brought the matter to a head when he confronted Semple. An argument broke out and Semple ordered his men to fire. Grant's men returned the fire. In the next few minutes, Semple, nineteen colonists and one Métis were killed. The Battle of Seven Oaks was over, but the damage it caused had only begun.

Lord Selkirk had arrived in Montreal a few months earlier to try uniting the Hudson's Bay Company and the Nor'Westers. He offered the Nor'Westers the right to trade in Athabaska and ship their goods through Hudson Bay on condition that, among other considerations, the Nor'Westers recognize the Bay's charter.

McGillivray countered. The North West Company had explored the country, mapped it and established the first posts there. He thought it would be fairer if the companies united, with the Bay taking one third of the shares and the Nor'Westers the remaining two thirds. Selkirk refused. The discussion ended.

Before leaving for England, Selkirk had asked for armed forces to protect his Red River Settlement. The authorities saw no need for such a move. They did not want armed warfare. Once again Selkirk moved on his own. He hired a troop of a hundred fighting men and a group of voyageurs to transport them, along with a boatload of arms and a furnace he had bought in Detroit for the purpose of making cannon balls.

On August 12, 1816, Selkirk's army appeared on the Kaministikwia River and camped across the river from Fort William. The next day an armed guard arrived at Fort William with a warrant for McGillivray's arrest on the grounds of treason, conspiracy and accessory to murder.

McGillivray, accompanied by Kenneth McKenzie and Dr. John McLoughlin, paddled over to Selkirk's camp to try and make sense out of what seemed a growing nightmare. Selkirk ordered all three arrested. Then he sent troops to Fort William, arresting fifteen more partners and seizing the fort.

During the night, the partners burned company records as fast as they could. On August 19, Selkirk placed McGillivray and the other partners, with the exception of Daniel McKenzie, along with as many company records as he could find, into canoes to be taken back to Montreal. The canoes were dangerously overloaded. McGillivray asked Selkirk to use some of the North West Company's canoes to reduce the loads. Selkirk refused. The brigade ran into a storm on Lake Superior, one canoe was swamped and nine Nor'Westers, including Kenneth McKenzie, were drowned in the windswept waters.

Selkirk notified Sir John Coape Sherbrooke, governor-general of Upper Canada, that he was sending "...a Cargo of Criminals of a larger caliber than usually came before the court of York..." and added that he was pleased to be able to tie up a large part of the North West Company's funds.

McGillivray, too, was concerned about those funds. The warehouses at Fort William were full of the season's packs. Prime pelts, valued at over £100,000 pounds, awaited shipment to Montreal.

There were other problems. A new American law forbade any but American citizens from trading with Indians on American territory. The South West Company had been put out of business. Astor bought the company in a forced sale at far less than its true value. These and other events left the North West Company in a serious financial position. McGillivray had every reason to worry.

McGillivray applied for a warrant for Selkirk's arrest, but Selkirk, surrounded by his hired army, ignored it. British North America's fur trade was in an uproar and far away in London, a two-man commission was finally appointed to look into the situation.

Tokens issued by the North West Company. The head of King George IV is on one side of the token.
Hudson's Bay Company Archives / Provincial Archives of Manitoba

Nicholas Garry, shown resting at Slave Falls, became a stockholder and member of the committee of the Hudson's Bay Company in 1817. In 1821, he accompanied Simon McGillivray to the Hudson's Bay territories to finalize arrangements for the union of the North West Company and the Hudson's Bay Company. Later, he served as deputy governor of the HBC. Fort Garry is named in his honour.

Hudson's Bay Company Archives / Provincial Archives of Manitoba

William McGillivray gloomily read reports from the field as Selkirk's soldiers seized Rainy Lake, then Fort Douglas, and plundered Bas de la Rivière Winnipic, the largest of the North West Company's inland provisioning depots. It was March, 1818, before the tangled situation between Selkirk and the North West Company finally came before the courts. There were hundreds of pages of evidence dealing with almost 180 separate charges. When the hearings finally ended, there was only one conviction against the Nor'Westers. Charles de Reinhard was sentenced to hang for the murder of Owen Keveny. Lord Selkirk was later fined £500 for resisting arrest at Fort William. Daniel McKenzie sued Selkirk for false arrest and was awarded £1,500.

The lawsuits may have been settled, but the problems had not gone away. Settlers remained on the Red River. Hudson's Bay Company brigades plunged deeper into Athabaska country. The old rivalry flared up, more fiercely than ever before.

Despite successes in the field, conditions continued to deteriorate for the North West Company. During the summer of 1819 they were desperate for working capital. More than ever, union with HBC seemed the only solution to NWC's problems. McGillivray returned to Canada, hoping that at last the two companies could come to terms. McGillivray's brother, Simon, and Edward Ellice, one of the NWC's important financial backers, continued to work in London, meeting with Andrew Colvile, Lord Selkirk's brother-in-law, who acted for the Bay.

While negotiations were going on, McGillivray discovered conditions were even worse than he had suspected. There was open hostility everywhere between HBC and NWC employees. Things were especially tense in Athabaska.

McGillivray's hopes for a peaceful settlement suddenly evaporated when Colvile turned cold and backed away from the negotiations. McGillivray was shocked when he learned the reason.

Nearly two years earlier, an unhappy group of wintering partners decided the Montreal partners weren't doing enough to straighten out the situation, so they had taken matters into their own hands. While McGillivray's representatives were in London making one offer to the Hudson's Bay Company, representatives of the unhappy traders also appeared, asking for a different sort of agreement. Colvile realized there was a split between the Montreal partners and the wintering partners, and played one side against the other.

Finally, on March 26, 1821, Simon McGillivray and Edward Ellice signed an agreement on behalf of the Nor'Westers combining the two companies. The union would carry on under the name of the Hudson's Bay Company. The two would share equally in putting up capital and would divide profits and losses equally. A joint board, made up of two members of each of the former companies and the governor (or deputy-governor) of the Hudson's Bay Company would advise on management of the fur trade.

There were mutterings of discontent, but the deal was completed. On July 15, 1821, James Leith, the first Nor'Wester to join the new Hudson's Bay Company, left for the Athabaska territory. Behind him the last meeting at Fort William came to an end as the last great Summer Rendezvous drew to a close.

Once again Indian trappers and traders faced a monopoly which would crush independent traders and drive fur prices down. This time the giant's grasp extended not only to Rupert's Land but all the way to the Pacific Coast.

When William McGillivray died in London, four years later, an era ended.

Simon McGillivray from a portrait by R. Remagle.
Hudson's Bay Company Archives / Provincial Archives of Manitoba

Chapter Five

George Simpson, Emperor of the North

George Simpson was a remarkable man. He was born in Scotland. The date of his birth is uncertain, but is believed to be about 1787. His parents were not married. Young George was raised by his father's sister, Mary Simpson, in a small port town in the northern Highland county of Ross. The boy was intelligent, worked hard at school and was a good student. One of the subjects he liked best was mathematics and, not surprisingly, his marks were good. His uncle, Geddes Mackenzie Simpson, was so impressed with the boy that he offered an apprenticeship at his sugar brokerage. Geddes was a partner in Graham and Simpson in London and the position meant a move to London. Simpson, now a teenager, was excited at the prospect of leaving his quiet Highland home for the lively and adventurous world of London. He worked hard in the brokerage, completed his apprenticeship and rose through the ranks of the company.

In 1812 the firm expanded and took in a new partner, Andrew Wedderburn. No record exists to explain what Wedderburn did next, but for some reason he changed his name from Wedderburn to Colvile. His sister, Jean Wedderburn, was married to Lord Selkirk. Colvile used this family connection to begin an impressive career with the Hudson's Bay Company.

As a new partner, Colvile wanted to make his mark, and kept a careful eye on company activities. He was impressed by George Simpson's application and by his intelligence. Simpson quickly demonstrated that he understand not only the "what" of business routines, but also the "why", and was able to think for himself.

Opposite: It often took brute strength to manoeuvre through the raging rapids, as depicted in this famous painting by Frances Anne Hopkins.
National Archives of Canada, #C-002774

In 1820 Colvile suggested Simpson for the position of acting overseas governor of the Hudson's Bay Company in Canada. He would head the organization until the merger between the old Hudson's Bay Company and the North West Company was completed, and the new Hudson's Bay Company solidly established. The 33-year-old Simpson accepted and set off for Canada just five days later.

His ship docked at New York. Simpson hired an open carriage for the trip from New York to Montreal, covering the distance in only seven days, despite a spring thaw that turned the rutted dirt roads into a soupy mess. Spills and accidents were frequent but unlike most other, more prudent travellers, Simpson refused to allow them to stay his progress.

The trip was typical of Simpson. In later years he became both feared and famous for his sudden and speedy journeys to Company posts. Of all the Bay's overseas governors, none came close to him in making on-site visits. He could turn up anywhere, from the most isolated post in Labrador to a far-off trading fort in New Caledonia. His paddlers were pushed to the limit and often beat seasoned voyageurs along the route. But if Simpson expected 100 percent performance from those who worked for him, he demanded no less of himself. His workload was huge but he gave his complete attention to everything he did.

His reports were precise, accurate and easy to read, but very much to the point. Simpson didn't allow himself time for pleasantries or gossip. His letters were polite, but dealt only with business. This was a man who was as direct in his thoughts as he was in his actions. Simpson's attention to detail was partly responsible for guiding the difficult negotiations between the Hudson's Bay Company and the North West Company to a successful conclusion. When the final document was signed, it guaranteed continued use of the Hudson's Bay Company name, provided a board that was weighted in the Bay's favour, and included a 21-year renewal clause.

Soon after, Simpson was named overseas governor, no longer simply acting in that capacity. It was a major achievement for such a young man, but for George Simpson it was only a beginning.

He began with a series of reforms to reduce costs. He ordered traders to replace presents of fancy clothing, beads, bells and other ornaments, with smaller gifts of tea, tobacco, sugar, flour, rice and raisins, and discouraged any trades or gifts involving alcohol. Next, Simpson carefully considered the operating statements of the 173 trading posts scattered across the Bay's far-flung empire and closed those which would interfere with each other. Many were former North West Company posts.

The Council of the Northern Department of Rupert's Land, meeting at Norway House, June 21, 1836, George Simpson presiding. Hudson's Bay Company Archives / Provincial Archives of Manitoba

The "amalgamation" was proving a hollow victory for the Nor'Westers. Ten years earlier, The North West Company had controlled 78 percent of Canadian fur sales. They ruled the Northwest and formed the first major Canadian establishment. Too-rapid expansion, internal squabbles and plain bad luck had led to their collapse. Now they held a lesser position in the amalgamation of the two companies. But worse was yet to come.

Fort William, the pride of the North West empire, with its enormous Great Hall and bustling square, was downgraded. As it was outside Rupert's Land, it could no longer be used for council meetings. When Fort William became just another supply depot, HBC's Norway House, second in importance only to York Factory, became the inland distribution centre.

65

Sir George Simpson in his later years.
Glenbow Archives

Now Simpson was ready to begin streamlining the organization. After reducing the number of trading posts the Company operated, he reorganized administration of the fur trade, making it more efficient. He began by dividing the Company's business into three departments: Montreal, Southern and Northern. The Montreal Department included Upper and Lower Canada, the King's Posts along the north shore of the Gulf of St. Lawrence and, later, Labrador. The Southern Department included part of the eastern shore of Hudson Bay and the territory between James Bay and the Montreal Department, along with the depot at Moose Factory, one of the first of the Hudson's Bay trading posts. The Northern Department covered the territory between Hudson Bay and the mountains, between the United States and the Arctic Ocean, and territory west of the Rocky Mountains. The divisions were made according to access routes by boat or canoe.

But despite all Simpson's changes, he was unable to alter the basic structure of the Hudson's Bay Company. Its reliance on the Home Board in London remained unchanged. It was this factor, perhaps more than any other, which irked the former North West Company partners. Accustomed to making their own decisions, or consulting with their partners in Montreal, the former Nor'Westers found the wait for responses or approval from a Board in far-away London both tiring and frustrating.

The 1821 coalition lasted for just three years. In 1824 the original profit-sharing agreement was cancelled and former North West Company partners were issued common stock instead of the preferred stock that Hudson's Bay Company partners received. The Nor'Westers no longer had a vote and now had almost no influence on Company decisions and policies.

George Simpson was firmly at the helm and he ran a tight ship.

TRAVELLING FROM LACHINE TO YORK FORT

George Simpson's new wife, Frances, recorded a typical morning on this trip. "At 2 a.m. the voyageurs were 'roused by Mr. Simpson's well-known call of 'Lève, Lève, Lève'; ... [Get up, Get up , Get up] ... the canoes were then laden and we embarked at 3 o'clock" and travelled, with a portage or two thrown in, until breakfast at 9 a.m.

"...our voyageurs... paddled, sang, laughed, and joked until one of them... seemed to feel the force of a joke ... which gave rise to a battle in the canoe. Mr. Simpson was asleep at the time but the noise awoke him and a shower of blows with a paddle... brought about an immediate cessation of hostility."

It was easy to dislike the man. He had many enemies and detractors, both in and out of the Company. He was direct, forthright and blunt. He brooked no interference and listened to few other people. The word "workaholic" had not yet been coined, but it describes George Simpson perfectly.

Part of his furious drive may have come from Calvinist influences which were prevalent in the Highlands during Simpson's youth. Calvinists were a hard-working, self-disciplined and frugal group, who stood out in a nation noted for hard work, discipline and frugality. In many ways, Simpson's actions in later life reflect their beliefs. But what made him such a complex person was his questioning attitude. He was not content to do something simply because that was the way it had always been done. "Good enough" did not count with Simpson. He wanted to find a better way to do everything that came within his grasp. Some of his ideas were progressive, beneficial and even visionary.

His study of the beaver was a case in point. Simpson knew the history of the beaver, knew of its virtual extinction in Europe, and could see the results of over-trapping in Canada. The success of the Company depended on the fur trade and most especially on the beaver. The profit margin for each trading post was critically important, so Simpson tried to find ways to improve that margin. Before trade could increase, the depleted stocks of beaver had to be replenished. This was a completely new attitude for European traders.

One of his first moves was attempting to persuade Indians not to trap beaver during the summer when the pelts were poor, nor to take cub beaver during the winter. Deciding that steel traps were too efficient, he encouraged Indians to use older, less-effective methods of trapping, such as the deadfall, so the beaver population could rebuild itself.

Neither move was very successful. In many districts food was scarce. Indians took beaver whenever they could. Whether the pelts were worth trading or not, the beaver itself was valuable for food. And in the Indian villages, even lower quality pelts were useful in everyday life.

RUSSIA'S AMERICAN COMPANY

Like France and England, Russia realized huge profits from North American furs. Russia's royal house subsidized exploration until 1743, when financial problems struck the royal treasury.

The Russian American Company was formed in 1799 to overcome the rivalries that were destroying individual traders. There were numerous settlements in Russian America, better known today as Alaska. These included Illiuliuk (Unalaska), St. Paul Harbour (Kodiak), New Russia (Yakutat), Novo-arkhangel'sk (Sitka), Unalakit, Ikogmiut and Nulato.

The pattern of over-trapping repeated itself in Alaska and by 1795 only three trading groups survived, led by Grigori Shelikhov, Pavel Sergevich Lebedev-Lastonchkin, and the Kiselev brothers. The Russian trade was based principally on sea otter, but also included beaver, seals and other marine animals.

Simpson's plans failed to take into consideration one of the basic facts of nature. The populations of most fur-bearing animals are not stable. They often run in cycles and these cycles are affected by many other factors. Fox, for example, eat many times their own weight in small rodents, such as mice. If something happens to the mouse population — and it can be affected by floods, drought or disease — the fox population is also affected.

During a low cycle, when pelts are scarce, traders usually gave trappers enough credit to carry them through until a good year came around. Then the trappers could clear up their bills. That was well and good as long as the trading posts stayed open from one year to the next. Under Simpson's new decrees, that no longer happened. He shifted trade from one area to another, staffing centres where trading was up, closing centres where trading was down. A closed trading post could not grant credit or provide supplies.

Simpson's actions can be seen from two points of view. On the one hand, they were a way of managing a renewable resource, one of the earliest recorded attempts at wildlife management in North America.

On the other hand, they created hardship and misery for many Indian trappers, who were by now dependent on the Company for both their income and their supplies. Simpson saw the advantages of diversification and tried to encourage them to widen their activities, but he was fighting a long-established tradition.

One of the complaints against the old Hudson's Bay Company had been its practice of using "made beaver" (a cured pelt) as a standard of exchange. Early traders equated all pelts with beaver — one mink, marten or otter skin counted for exactly the same as one beaver skin, despite the fact that the mink, marten and otter were worth far more than beaver at the fur auctions in England. Now, when Simpson wanted trappers to search for pelts other than beaver, he had to pay premium prices for those pelts. Even so, trappers preferred beaver. It provided both food and pelts. Mink, marten and many other fur-bearers did not.

Simpson's next move was imposing quotas and, in 1826, trappers in the Northern Department were allowed to bring out only a certain number of pelts for trading. The Company couldn't impose quotas in some districts, such as the lower Red River or Lac la Pluie, because American traders were nearby. If the Company tried to enforce a quota there, trappers could simply fill their quotas with the Company, then take their surplus pelts to trade with the Americans. The danger to that was that the Americans might, and likely would, encourage them to bring in all of their pelts and forget about trading with the Company. In areas where the quota system could be enforced, fur harvests were reduced to between 20 percent and 50 percent of previous totals. This created real hardship for Native trappers who had few alternate sources of income.

Simpson protected the Bay's interests with all the savage ferocity of a pitbull terrier. He was determined that his portion of the Bay's empire would be a shining example of good stewardship and good management.

At that time, the Bay had an extensive empire. It had trading posts in Russian America (Alaska) and the Sandwich Islands (Hawaii). But the bulk of its holdings were in North America. They stretched from Labrador to the Pacific Coast, dipped down to include a trading post in San Francisco and jointly occupied, with the fledgling United States government, the present-day states of Oregon, Washington, Idaho, Wyoming and Montana.

Many historians agree that the North West Company was the forerunner of Canadian confederation. It was the North West Company that explored and mapped the vast areas of Western Canada. These explorations led in turn to the establishment of trading posts as far south as the Oregon Territories and as far west as British Columbia. They formed the groundwork for Britain's claims in Western Canada.

Once the North West Company and the Hudson's Bay Company amalgamated, Simpson's actions in consolidating and strengthening the Company's position in these areas gave greater weight to Britain's claims and ultimately helped prevent the western provinces from being absorbed into the United States.

Chapter Six
Labrador Smith

By all odds, James Douglas should have become simply one more unnoticed worker in the sugar fields of British Guiana, South America. A combination of factors changed his life and helped Douglas forge an important place in the history of Canada.

He was the son of John Douglas, a Glasgow merchant who owned sugar estates in Demerara, British Guiana. His mother was Martha Ritchie, the daughter of a black freedwoman from Barbados. His parents were not married. That was not an unusual circumstance in that time and place. What was unusual was that John Douglas did not simply leave the child to be raised by its mother and to work in the cane fields.

Douglas took an active interest in his son's future and sent the boy to Lanark School in Scotland and then to a boarding school at Chester.

There is some question about when Douglas was born and when he joined the North West Company. From information now available, it appears he was born sometime around August 15, 1803, and joined the North West Company in 1819, when he was either 15 or 16 years of age.

Douglas spent two years with the North West Company. He was a good worker and appears to have been well liked. When the fur companies amalgamated in 1821, he entered the service of the new Hudson's Bay Company and was eventually sent to the New Caledonia District of the Western Department, where he served as a clerk at Fort St. James under William Connolly. Connolly and his wife had a pretty, teen-aged daughter named Amelia. Before long, Amelia won Douglas's heart and in 1824 they were married. Six years later Douglas was transferred. He and Amelia moved to one of the Company's newest posts, Fort Vancouver.

Opposite: The famous artist, Frederic Remington, depicts Native people bringing in furs to negotiate a sale, 1860.
Glenbow Archives

In the 1830s the Company was firmly in control of the fur trade in Oregon, but control of the land itself was still in dispute. Britain and the United States signed an agreement of joint occupancy, which was renewed in 1827 for a ten-year term. At the end of that time, they hoped to come to an agreement that would settle the question once and for all.

Around this time, the Company decided to move its trading fort some distance up the Columbia River. The river does not flow in a straight line, however, and while the Company moved up the river, they moved quite a bit deeper into the disputed territory. On the northern bank of the river, across from Hayden Island, they built Fort Vancouver. Today it sits on the southern border of the State of Washington, just across the river from Oregon.

Fort Vancouver was a vital part of the Company's empire until James Polk, president of the United States, with his vision of manifest destiny, re-opened negotiations with Britain. In 1846 the land was ceded and the boundary moved north to the 49th parallel.

The Company may have guessed that its position at Fort Vancouver was not very secure. Before the boundary was officially relocated they built a new fort on the southern tip of Vancouver Island. It was first called Fort Camosun, then Fort Albert and on June 10, 1843, was officially named Fort Victoria, in honour of the young queen of England.

Around this time, the Church of Latter Day Saints (Mormons) from Utah contacted London asking for land grants on Vancouver Island.

The request was refused. Instead, Britain gave the whole of Vancouver Island to the Hudson's Bay Company, and made them responsible for colonizing the island.

Douglas had done well at Fort Vancouver and when the Company moved to Fort Victoria, he was placed in charge of what was now the headquarters for the Columbia District. In 1851 he was appointed Governor of Vancouver Island, a position he held until 1863. Surprisingly, when the appointment was made he was not asked to give up his position with the Hudson's Bay Company. He continued in both roles until 1858, when he was appointed Governor of the Colony of British Columbia.

Douglas is credited with saving British Columbia from invasion and possible annexation by the Americans, when the 1858 Gold Rush sent thousands of miners to the Fraser River.

In the 1860s, he ordered a roadway built to serve miners heading for the Cariboo. It was a corduroy road, built of logs, but it kept the traffic moving — and what traffic there was! Teams of mules, oxen, horses and even camels hauled freight along the busy route. Wagons carried cargo ranging from gold pans and shovels to a grand piano. Douglas's corduroy road was the lifeline for Cariboo miners, settlers, government officials, travelling salesmen and a thousand others drawn like iron filings by the magnetic lure of gold.

His lifetime of service was rewarded when he was called to London to be knighted. In 1864 he returned to Victoria — and the Bay boardroom — as Sir James Douglas.

Meanwhile, yet another Scot was about to enter the Hudson's Bay Company limelight.

Donald Alexander Smith was born in 1820, at Forres, in Scotland. As a young boy, he was hired by the town clerk, Robert Watson. He spent most of his time copying documents. It was dull work, but Smith stuck with it. His life was brightened considerably when his uncle, John Stuart, arrived in Forres. Stuart was a former Nor'Wester, who had been second-in-command on Simon Fraser's exploration of the Fraser River. John Stuart spun many tales of this and other voyages, which made his young nephew's head reel with excitement and his heart ache at the prospect of copying more documents in Robert Watson's office.

Stuart offered to write a letter of recommendation to George Simpson. On the strength of that, Smith walked from Forres to Aberdeen where he boarded a schooner to London. He found a ship destined for Canada and on May 16, 1838, set sail on the *Royal William* with almost nothing in his pocket but a handful of letters.

From Montreal he walked to the Company offices at Lachine and introduced himself to Simpson, quickly handing over his uncle's letter of recommendation.

Simpson admired the young man's determination and hired the boy as an apprentice clerk. He was put to work in the company warehouse at Lachine. Sorting muskrat pelts in a huge, dusty building wasn't quite the dashing, glamorous life Smith had imagined, but he stayed at it, learning all he could about this strange new trade.

He also used his uncle's other letters of introduction, which brought him into the exciting social life of Montreal. Smith enjoyed himself immensely, but it seems he trod on some very important toes, including the knobby appendages of the Governor, George Simpson. Smith was transferred to Tadoussac, on the Gulf of St. Lawrence.

Tadoussac was a very old trading centre. It was outside of the Company's area of monopoly. Trapping was poor, trading was slow, and there was stiff competition for every pelt that was brought in. Tadoussac was rich in history — it was the site of Jacques Cartier's first fur-trading mission in 1535. But history was of little consolation to the unhappy young man who desperately missed the excitement and activity of Montreal.

A few years later he was put in charge of Mingan, a remote location at the mouth of the Mingan River, which flows into the lower St. Lawrence north of Anticosti Island. Mingan was even more isolated than Tadoussac.

With little to do, Smith seems to have done even less than was required. In 1845, George Simpson appeared for a surprise inspection. The post's account books were in terrible shape. Simpson, with his love for clear entries and balanced numbers, was furious. Smith resolved to do better, but things went from bad to worse. The next year, he did try to keep better ledgers but shortly before his reports were due the post burned down, destroying Smith's ledgers. Simpson was not amused.

Moose Factory was one of the HBC's earliest settlements, dating back to its choice as a centre for trade in the Bay region as early as 1673.
Drawing by W. Trask, 1854. Hudson's Bay Company Archives / Provincial Archives of Manitoba

In a thoroughly untypical gesture, Simpson gave the young man one more chance. Chief Trader William Nourse was in charge of the area near what is now Goose Bay/Happy Valley, on the North West River, in Labrador. Nourse fell ill. Simpson sent James Grant to Labrador to relieve him. Donald Smith was to be Grant's assistant. When Grant moved to North West River, Smith was temporarily placed in charge of the post at Rigolet, in Hamilton Inlet.

In September, Nourse's successor, Chief Trader Richard Hardisty, arrived. Smith was demoted back to clerk and remained in that position until Hardisty went out on leave.

Largely due to Hardisty's support, Smith was promoted in 1852 and put in charge of the Esquimaux Bay District. When Hardisty and his wife left, their daughter, Isabella, remained at North River with her husband, James Grant.

Company officials could perform marriages in the area covered by the Charter, just as ship captains can perform marriages at sea. Labrador, though, was outside the Bay's Charter area. When Isabella's father performed the marriage ceremony between his daughter and James Grant, it was not legal. Within a few years, James and Isabella separated and Isabella and Donald Smith decided to marry.

If her first wedding was unusual, Isabella's second was even more so. Smith said he had been appointed a lay preacher by the Governor of Newfoundland and therefore was entitled to perform marriages. He presided at his own wedding.

Donald Smith spent twenty years in Labrador and used his time well. He carved a seven-acre farm out of the wilderness, planted a large garden and raised chickens, sheep and cattle, to provide for his family. He was determined to show high returns in the fur trade, but wanted profits from other sources as well. He opened a fish cannery and began exporting barrels of seal oil.

*A*t this time, the Company made a change that was to have profound effects on Smith's future. Control of Labrador and Newfoundland had been a problem for many years. In 1763, Newfoundland had been awarded all of the coastal area, and the territory of Labrador. In 1825 the North Shore was restored to Lower Canada (now Quebec).

In 1855, London separated Newfoundland from Upper and Lower Canada and gave it the right to responsible government. At the same time, the Company separated Labrador from the Lachine area. This meant that Smith now dealt directly with headquarters in London.

Sometime during these years, he became known as "Labrador Smith", possibly to distinguish him from other Smiths. Labrador Smith made profits for the Company, but he ensured his own future at the same time. As early as 1853 he began buying stocks, beginning with two shares in the Bank of Montreal.

Smith's benefactor, George Simpson, died in 1860. His successor, Alexander Grant Dallas, moved Company headquarters from Montreal to Red River, which then became the centre of the Company's trade. Little was left in Montreal, but when E. M. Hopkins, Chief Factor of the Montreal District, retired Labrador Smith replaced him.

In 1864, Smith took home leave. It was his first trip back to Scotland in 16 years. After visiting his mother, he returned to London and spent the rest of his vacation at Company headquarters. There he met the Governor, Sir Edmund Walker Head, and other influential officials. When his leave ended, he returned to Montreal.

In 1869 Canada was made up of only four provinces: Nova Scotia, New Brunswick, and a Quebec and Ontario which were much smaller than their present-day versions. The Government of Canada wanted to enlarge its territory and began negotiations with Britain. Rupert's Land would be returned to the Crown in return for £300,000 in compensation. The Company could continue its trade in Canada and would receive land grants amounting to 18,275 hectares around its trading posts. In addition, they would have the option to claim nearly seven million acres (2,832,200 hectares) between Lake Winnipeg and the Rocky Mountains. The Company didn't have to make any quick decisions on the land claims — the option was to remain open for 50 years.

The Company accepted.

LOUIS RIEL — FOUNDING FATHER OR TREASONOUS REBEL?

Louis Riel was freed into exile. Elected to parliament, he was unable to take his seat; granted amnesty, he was forbidden to return to Canada until 1880. He settled in Montana but was persuaded to come back to help the Saskatchewan River Métis in the second North West Rebellion. In defeat, he was executed for treason, despite the fact that he had become an American citizen.

At this time, the Canadian West was sparsely populated and very isolated. There were only three ways to reach it: the traditional voyageur route along the rivers, the Hudson's Bay route from York Factory, or the Red River cart track that pushed northward from Minnesota. Even though it was not easy to reach, settlers began to move in. Soon one of the largest centres of population west of Canada was near Fort Garry, the Hudson's Bay Company post near the junction of the Red and Assiniboine rivers, and the site of modern-day Winnipeg.

The district soon began negotiations to join Canada. William McDougall, Minister of Public Works in the first government of Sir John A. Macdonald, sent surveyors to chart the Red River territory. The surveyors began to lay out square townships, some falling directly across the long, river-front acres farmed by the Métis. A young man appeared from the settlement, stepped on their chains to prevent further surveying, and sent them away. The young man was named Louis Riel. He and other Métis formed a committee to discuss the problem and decide on a course of action.

McDougall had just been named the first lieutenant-governor of the North West Territories, effective December 1, 1869. He decided to set out for his new domain a little early, to look around before he took office. He arrived at the Customs House in Dakota Territory on October 30, ready to make his entry into the North West Territories, but was stopped at the boundary of Rupert's Land.

A few days earlier, Riel had seized Fort Garry. William McTavish, in charge of the fort, was close to death with tuberculosis. Riel placed him under house arrest. There was no opposition when Riel declared himself President of the Provisional Government of Rupert's Land and the North West Territories. Almost immediately, a group of Americans invited Riel to bring the North West Territories into the United States.

When word of this reached Sir John A. Macdonald, he took the logical step of contacting the Company's headquarters to find out what was going on. He did not know the headquarters had been moved and, as usual, contacted the Company's representative in Montreal. He reached Donald A. Smith.

Smith was happy to give Macdonald the benefit of his opinions. And to add that he was completely impartial. In truth, he didn't know enough about the situation to have an opinion on it. Macdonald, unaware of the true state of Smith's involvement, asked him to go to Fort Garry and help settle the dispute. Smith agreed and set off, carrying the title of "Dominion Commissioner to Inquire into the North West Rebellion".

Smith met with Riel, who was not quite as easily taken in as Macdonald had been. He carefully examined Smith's documents before talks began. Riel decided Smith's appointment was genuine and set up a public forum.

Above: Donald Smith and Louis Riel at Fort Garry, 1870.
From the illustration by Bruce Johnson. Hudson's Bay Company Archives / PAM

On January 19, on a day as cold as only Winnipeg winters can produce, more than a thousand residents gathered in the open air to hear discussions between Riel and Smith. When the short daylight hours drew to a close, the meeting was adjourned until the next day. Soon after sunrise Smith continued, reading first from one document, then another, and eventually voicing his own opinions. During these two days, Riel translated Smith's words faithfully.

When Smith finished speaking, Riel suggested that a group of 20 Métis and 20 English-speaking representatives meet to consider Smith's presentation, and draw up a list of rights to submit to Ottawa — the Bill of Rights under which the people of the Red River were willing to join Canada. Riel was to continue as head of the provisional government.

Smith's mission seemed headed for success, when a group of malcontents from Portage la Prairie marched on the scene, determined to hang Riel.

There was a scuffle and a young settler, Hugh John Sutherland, was shot to death. Riel's riflemen arrested members of the gang, including an Irish Protestant named Thomas Scott. Scott began jeering and insulting his captors, harassing the Métis about their religion and culture, and generally disrupting events. At one point he physically attacked Riel. Scott was brought before a court martial. He was found guilty of insubordination and sentenced to death. The sentence was carried out on March 4, 1870.

Scott was not the first man to be sentenced to death at court martial for an offence that would today be little more than a misdemeanour. Nor would he be the last. But he was the first sentenced under Riel's provisional government, and an anti-Riel party seized on the incident. They whipped up public outrage, playing on traditional differences between Catholics and Protestants, and the cultural chasm between the British and the Métis.

Five days later, Bishop Taché arrived in the colony with a message from Macdonald. The Prime Minister would grant general amnesty and welcome Red River into Confederation as a province, to be called Manitoba. Three Red River delegates left for Ottawa to negotiate the terms of the Manitoba Act. It satisfied most of Riel's demands, including guarantees for the French language and Catholic religion, and set aside 1.4 million acres (566,580 hectares) for the Métis, retaining their traditional long lots along the river.

Meanwhile Sir John A. Macdonald dispatched troops to the Red River to keep the peace, and to bring Riel to task.

Riel was anxious to have peace keepers in the little settlement and welcomed their arrival. Believing he and his provisional government were included in Ottawa's amnesty, Riel arranged civil and military ceremonies to welcome their leader, Colonel Garnet Wolseley, and to officially hand over the provisional government.

Shortly before the troops arrived at Fort Garry, however, Riel learned the full extent of Wolseley's mission. He and his lieutenants withdrew across the river to St. Boniface, cutting the ferry cables behind them to prevent pursuit. Wolsely occupied an unprotected fort. It was a bitter day for the fledgling government, for the Red River Métis and for Riel personally.

Donald Smith was pressed into service as the interim head of government, a position he held until the arrival, on September 2, 1870, of Adams G. Archibald, the newly appointed Lieutenant-Governor of the Province of Manitoba.

At that point, Smith bowed out of local politics and returned to his home to resume his chores. It was time to streamline the Company. Smith had never served in the North West Territories and had little association with the Nor'Westers. He was not bound by the customs and traditions they had evolved. His Labrador roots had isolated him, but it was isolation with productive results. For example, when Smith looked at the Montreal canoes, the *canot du nord* and the York boats travelling to and from York Factory, he didn't see their glorious history. He saw inefficiency and needless expenditure of time, money and energy. Modern boats could be powered by machines, not men. Smith believed these new vessels would be a much better way to meet the Company's transportation needs.

A fleet of flat-bottomed sternwheeled steamboats replaced the canoes and York boats on the Saskatchewan, the Assiniboine and the Red rivers. Next, the long and painful Grand Rapids portages gave way to a four-mile long tramline, powered by a single white horse.

Sir Donald A. Smith, Baron Strathcona and Mount Royal, was Governor of the HBC, 1889-1914. He was the dominant personality in the Company during the late 19th century and early 20th century. His career spanned fur trading, member of parliament, principal investor in the CPR, Governor of the HBC and Canadian High Commissioner to Great Britain.

Hudson's Bay Company Archives / Provincial Archives of Manitoba

During the years that followed, Smith transformed the Company's focus from beaver pelts to real estate. In 1874, he formally resigned as a fur trade commissioner and became the Company's first land commissioner. He moved the main office from Winnipeg back to Montreal, but he kept a close eye on the area: under his direction a small hotel was built at Portage la Prairie, grist mills were built to serve the growing number of wheat farmers, and a ferry service was opened crossing the Assiniboine at Fort Ellice. The Company was widening its horizons.

Smith finally resigned as land commissioner in 1879. He was followed by Charles John Brydges, who had been general manager of the Grand Trunk Railway.

Over a 20-year period, Smith had greatly increased his personal holdings. He became a man of power and influence. He was a director with the Bank of Montreal and chief shareholder in the Royal Trust Company, and a major stockholder in the Canadian Pacific Railway. During this time, Eden Colvile, son of Deputy Governor Andrew Colvile, rose to a position of prominence in the Company. Colvile had been Associate Governor of Rupert's Land from 1849 until 1852, when he returned to London. He became Deputy Governor in 1871, remaining in that position until 1880, when he was named Governor. He retired on January 17, 1889.

THE NORTH WEST COMPANY

Donald Alexander Smith was elected to replace him. As both Governor of the Company and its largest stockholder, he was in a unique position of power. Smith had tasted political power during the Riel uprising, and enjoyed it. Now he turned his attention to provincial politics. He held a seat in Manitoba's first provincial election and was appointed to the executive council of the North West Territories. In 1871, Smith represented Selkirk in the House of Commons. He broke with Prime Minister Macdonald over the "Pacific Scandal" issue, helping to defeat the government. Later, he represented Montreal West from 1887 to 1896.

During Smith's terms of office, one of the main topics of Parliamentary discussion was British Columbia's decision to become Canada's sixth province. It was a conditional decision. British Columbia would enter Confederation only if it could be linked by rail to the rest of Canada within 10 years.

When the Canadian Pacific Railway was finally laid, connecting Montreal and Vancouver, it was Donald Smith who, on November 7, 1885, hammered the last spike at Craigellachie, British Columbia.

Smith returned to politics and, as the Tory member for Montreal West, was in the running as the man to replace Sir John A. Macdonald. But Smith's dreams were higher than that. He wanted to become Canada's High Commissioner to the Court of St. James in London, England. His dream came true. At the age of 76, Donald Alexander Smith, Governor of the Hudson's Bay Company, was named High Commissioner.

During the Royal Jubilee of 1897, Smith was given the title of Lord Strathcona. He had no difficulty choosing a crest. It was composed of familiar ingredients: the North West Company's beaver gnawing the base of a maple tree. His coat of arms included a canoe and paddlers. The motto was also familiar: NWC's "Perseverance". Only the last quartering was original — a hammer and nail, symbolizing the Craigellachie spike. It was ironic that he did not choose any portions of the Hudson's Bay Company coat of arms, but used instead the most significant parts from that of the North West Company.

Smith may have appeared tough-skinned, but this hard-necked Scot had one sensitive spot. He feared that word of possible irregularities of his marriage to Isabella would leak out, destroying his social standing and reputation. He had re-married Isabella twice already. Now, in a secret wedding at the British Embassy in Paris, the 77-year-old groom and his bride were married for the fourth time. He had finally laid his dragons to rest and stopped the possibility of scandal.

These were busy years for the Company. Still active in the fur trade, although on a lesser scale, it was now heavily involved in land development and transportation. Now it turned to retail development. In 1881 the Company built a genuine department store in Winnipeg, with small departments for drygoods, hardware and groceries.

In 1897, a new group of customers appeared. The Yukon's cry of "Gold in Bonanza Creek!" rang out across the country, setting into motion one of the largest and most exciting gold rushes ever seen in North America. Suddenly everyone dreamed of finding gold, and the would-be miners needed equipment. In many cases they were true Cheechakos — tenderfeet. Many had never camped out, had no idea of where they were going and even less notion of what to do once they got there. The Company's western trading posts made up lists of supplies for miners.

The Yukon gold rush soon ended, when another strike lured most of the miners away. The Company returned to its more traditional customers. Then, in what seemed like a re-run of the fur-trade days, a bustling upstart challenged the staid old company. Timothy Eaton's store took aim at the heart of the Hudson's Bay Company territory — Winnipeg — and created a spectacular department store in the centre of town.

Gradually the newcomer took business away from the Bay, just as the Nor' Westers had chiselled away at the edge of HBC trade. Eaton's worked on the basis of cash, instead of charge. It was bigger, brighter, and more aggressive. It quickly became a formidable competitor.

It took time, but by 1907 the giant began to stir, wakened by a new member of the HBC board, Leonard Cunliffe. Cunliffe appealed to Richard Burbidge, managing director of Harrods' of London, the world's most famous department store. Burbidge and Cunliffe set out on a voyage of discovery to Canada to find out exactly what was happening in the retail arm of the company.

They were not pleased with what they found. The stores were still being run as trading posts.

There was little merchandising, promotion or advertising. Customers had a limited selection of stock, and turn-over was slow. Old-fashioned accounting systems didn't help.

In his later years, HBC's Governor, Lord Strathcona, was against change. It took a shareholder revolt in 1910 to bring matters to a head. Thomas Skinner was promoted to Deputy Governor and four new directors took their seats, including the first-ever Canadian director. He brought the proud name of Mackenzie back into the firm. William Mackenzie was a former teacher who left the classroom to enter the world of business. He later became president of the Canadian Northern Railway.

The new board split the Company into separate departments for fur trading, land sales and retailing. As new blood began to course through the Bay's veins, it once again became a vital force on the Canadian retail scene. In 1913 new stores opened in Calgary and Vancouver. They would be the first of many.

At 93, Lord Strathcona was too old and too feeble to attend the openings. His last public function was the traditional Dominion Day reception on July 1st at Queen's Hall. Four months later, his beloved Isabella died at the age of 89. Smith outlived his bride by only 10 weeks. On January 21, 1914, at the age of 94, he died. To the last he was concerned about the status of his marriage, or rather his marriages, to Isabella. His deathbed statement explained once again that Isabella's first marriage (to Grant) had not been valid, and that he and Isabella had been legally joined.

Labrador Smith had devoted 76 years of his life to the Company. He was a remarkable man, and he left a remarkable record.

Chapter Seven
Times of Crisis and Stagnation

*I*n 1912, the Company's directors, in London, tried to help the firm regain its place in the Canadian market by appointing a Canadian-based advisory committee. Unfortunately, it was exactly that — an advisory committee with no authority. Too often, their advice fell on deaf ears. The basic problem remained: Head Office was too far away and reacted too slowly.

In 1914, Sir Robert Kindersley was named Governor. He had scarcely taken office when a worldwide crisis put Company problems in the shade. The First World War broke out and with that everything changed. Young men throughout the Commonwealth enlisted to fight the war that was to end all wars. Employees wanted to form a Company regiment of their own. That wasn't possible, but there were many other ways to help the war effort. It was in transportation, not manpower, that the Company made its strongest contribution.

In the more than two centuries since its formation, the Company had learned a lot about transportation. It learned how to find alternate methods of transportation, learned to be ingenious, and to be economical. It had also learned how to succeed in appalling conditions. Now it worked through a web of agencies to form a transportation network that would carry goods and supplies, troops and horses to and from the various fronts of war. Eventually the Company was responsible for a fleet of almost 300 merchant ships. It might not have been glamorous work, but it was essential. There was a very real degree of danger and on at least one occasion, a high degree of excitement as well.

Opposite: SS Nascopie *loading munitions at Brest, bound for Archangel, December 1916*
Hudson's Bay Company Archives / Provincial Archives of Manitoba

The Company's northern supply ship *Nascopie* was transporting supplies to the Russian army in Archangel, in 1917, when a German submarine surfaced nearby. Its commander ordered *Nascopie* to hand over its cargo or risk being shot. Company men had a long tradition of not handing over goods entrusted to their care. Captain G. Edmund Mack was not about to break that tradition. He would give up neither his ship nor his cargo. Instead, he ordered his deck gunner to fire on the submarine. Moments later, the sub slithered under the water. Legend has it that *Nascopie* made history as one of the first commercial transports to sink a German submarine.

The truth wasn't quite that exciting. *Nascopie*'s shots didn't sink the U-boat. In fact, War Department records show they didn't even hit it. But whether he sank the boat or not, Captain Mack's action saved the *Nascopie* and her cargo, and did wonders for her crew's morale.

When the war ended in 1918, the world was a different place. To many city-dwellers, and returning soldiers, the wide open spaces of the Canadian West seemed irresistible. By the thousands, settlers flocked to the Prairies, looking for places to call their own. It was a boom time for the Company's real estate division, and they made the most of it. In the post-war years they sold some 400,000 acres (162,000 hectares) at an average price of $15 per acre.

By this time there were three main divisions in the Company's corporate structure. The Land offices and the Fur Trade offices remained headquartered in eastern Canada. The Retail Division headed by Herbert E. Burbidge, whose father had been manager of Harrods' Department Store in London, broke away from the other two and moved to Vancouver. Before long, Burbidge was replaced by Edward Fitzgerald, who increased the authority of the Canadian Advisory Committee. After five years, Fitzgerald resigned.

Above: A fur press was used to compact the furs for bundling. This picture was taken about 1910. Hudson's Bay Company Archives / Provincial Archives of Manitoba

It was an eventful time for the Company. They were on the eve of their 250th anniversary, and decided to celebrate the event. Sir Robert Kindersley, the new Governor, came to Canada to take part. There was a spectacular gathering in Winnipeg.

Almost every Native group that had ever been associated with the Company was represented. There were chiefs from Hudson Bay, James Bay and Lake Winnipeg. There were delegations from the Peace, Athabaska, Pacific Slopes and Red River Valley. Non-Native groups included former employees, many retired, who travelled from all parts of the country to join the celebration. Almost everyone was in costume. They wore Native garb, voyageur outfits, Métis clothing, or old-fashioned clerk's garments. A mighty armada formed on the river. *Canot du nord*, Montreal canoes and York boats moved slowly past the old fort. Governor Kindersley acknowledged the groups as they passed by in review.

Then the speeches began, followed by music, merriment and feasting. When all the saluting was over, when the last dance was danced and the last toast drunk, Company employees had a chance to think about Kindersley's words. They made pleasant remembering. Every employee received a bonus of one month's salary. A pension plan was set in place. And Kindersley affirmed his faith in the future of the fur trade.

That was an important point. Many old-timers were alarmed at what was happening to their company. They felt it had lost its virility, excitement and sense of adventure. It seemed to be turning into just another chain of retail stores, and there was no sense of history in that. But even Kindersley may have been surprised by what happened next.

Above: York boats still were being used into the early twentieth century; seen here with canoes, about 1920. Provincial Archives of Manitoba

Attractive Styles in Ladies' Fur Sets

B882 $9.50

B883 $10.00

B878 $35.00

B881 $57.50

B877 $16.50

B880 $105.00

B875 $10.50

B879 $21.00

B876 $13.50

B874 $11.50

AN UNUSUAL STYLE ABOUT OUR FURS.

Not only is the quality of Fur all right but the style and Handsome Appearance leaves nothing to be desired.

When beaver was king, a broad belt across the middle of the country was the centre of activity. Other furs were valuable, but it was beaver that had built the business, and the best pelts came from that area. Mink and sable were luxury furs. Fox was a novelty. Along with ermine, raccoon and otter, they had limited markets.

Three things changed that. The first was the depletion of the beaver. In many areas the beaver was trapped out. Elsewhere, beavers were forced out as cities, towns and farms spread across land that was once home to vast amounts of wildlife. Conservation areas were established, but in many cases the fur harvest could not be restored.

The second event was the introduction of commercial fur farming. Independent fur farmers sold pelts, on commission, at the Company's fur auctions. This soon became a significant part of the Company's annual fur harvest.

The third event had to do with Hollywood. The fur trade has always been fickle and driven by fashion. Now moving pictures shaped the taste of fashionable women.

Colour had not yet arrived on movie screens and films were shot in black and white. Dark furs don't photograph well in this medium. They don't have the sleek, luxurious appearance they have in real life. They tend to absorb light and have a "heavy" look which detracts from the wearer. Pale furs, on the other hand, reflect light, photograph superbly and bathe their wearers in a glamorous glow. Silver fox was the fur of choice for the blonde beauties of the silver screen. And this new "look" opened a whole new window of fashion. Suddenly, white fox became the fur of choice. The finest came from the Arctic tundra.

A close second in popularity were the little red Arctic foxes from the Northern forests. Fashionable women draped red fox neckpieces over their shoulders wherever and whenever possible, topping dresses, suit jackets or coats. The fox's glass bead eyes kept glittering watch while its taxidermy teeth clutched its tail, holding the circlet of furs snugly in place. It didn't matter that California temperatures might be in the high 80s, or that New York and Washington reeled under high humidity. Women happily sweltered rather than remove their fur coats, jackets or neckpieces.

Above: Samples of the HBC's fur goods from the Winter catalogue of 1920-21.
Hudson's Bay Company Archives / Provincial Archives of Manitoba.

The Company had always had a few northern outposts, but they were very small and extremely isolated. Now, the northern business was the focal point of the boom in both red and silver fox. One of the important centres was Kuujjuak, the oldest of the Company's Far North posts. Kuujjuak, known for many years as Fort Chimo, had been in operation since 1830. From the middle of the 19th century, it was the centre of a prosperous commerce in whaling. Early whalers from Davis Strait and Baffin Bay moved to the more protected northern waters of Hudson Bay.

For a few years, whales seemed a limitless resource. They were not. By the end of the 1800s, overkill had taken its toll. The waters were "whaled-out", just as southern valleys had been "beavered-out". At the same time, demand for whale products dropped. Whale-bone corsets no longer crimped the waists of fashionable women.

Kerosene replaced whale oil. Palm and coconut oils took their place in margarine manufacturing. Soon whalers and independent traders left. Around the bay, old trading stations fell into disuse and disrepair as one by one they were abandoned. When the demand for fox and seal brought new commercial interest to Inuit lands, the Company moved quickly, renovating and re-opening old posts.

Many Inuit still lived in the old way, using traditional methods to harvest the bounty of land and sea. Vast herds of barren-ground caribou still roamed the northlands, following their migratory paths between the Northern tree line and the Arctic Ocean. Fish and seal were important parts of Inuit diets. But older methods of trapping and hunting were not as productive as the newer ways, and Inuit quickly turned to the steel traps, guns and ammunition available in the Company posts.

HBC store interior, Bathurst Inlet, circa 1939.
Hudson's Bay Company Archives,
Provincial Archives of Manitoba

Beaver House, London, England, headquarters of the HBC, opened in 1925.
Hudson's Bay Company Archives / Provincial Archives of Manitoba

While the southern department struggled against increasingly stiff retail competition, the northern department continued in splendid isolation. New furs became popular: polar bear hides, Arctic wolf and weasel increased the scope of Inuit hunters and trappers. But the new prosperity brought a new set of problems.

Traders introduced the idea of private ownership. It was a difficult and unsettling concept for the Inuit, whose culture was based on sharing. There were other problems as well. Many Inuit acquired a taste for imported goods. Metal knives, metal pots, tea, tobacco and sugar were luxuries at first, but soon people came to rely on them.

While the Far North struggled with its problems, the Company celebrated the new boom in furs. The Hudson's Bay Company marked its 255th anniversary on May 2, 1925, by opening a new head office and auction house, Beaver House, on Great Trinity Lane in London.

The new interest in Arctic and Northern furs brought a steady growth in business, but they were not the Company's only northern concerns. Gas and oil also offered exciting areas of growth.

There had been a vague interest in oil since the late 1800s, when crews drilling for water in southern Alberta found gas instead. At the time, it was only a nuisance to the drilling crews, who had to search elsewhere for water. Athabaska's tar sands were not unknown. Early fur traders, including the intrepid Peter Pond, learned of them from Indian guides, but for years they were little more than a curiosity. Except for patching canoes and limited medicinal applications, no one could find anything useful to do with the tar sands except to coat roads — and there were very few roads in that part of Canada.

Lord Strathcona had been a wily business man. At times, his far-sighted and shrewd moves were underestimated by his colleagues and competitors. At one point in his career, Strathcona was chairman of both the Burma Oil Company and the Anglo-Persian Oil Company. He encouraged the search for oil in Canada and kept a keen eye on the results. Well aware of the potential value of gas and oil, he insisted that the Company retain mineral rights on land it sold. His foresight was to be richly rewarded in years to come.

A century earlier, the Royal Navy, searching for a reliable source of power, had switched from sail to coal. Now they converted from coal to oil, eliminating the hours-long process of bringing coal-burning engines up to speed. Oil also eliminated the long, back-breaking stops to re-fill coal bunkers. There was, however, a major drawback.

Britain had no oil reserves. She was forced to buy oil from other nations. During times of war, supplies could suddenly dwindle or dry up completely. The Admiralty searched desperately for supplies of oil in a land it could depend upon. Canada's oil offered that potential.

The Company had come a long way from the fur trade. Oil, gas, land sales and retail stores were part of the diversification that marked its modern activities, and increased the value of its shares. Robert Kindersley was pleased with its growth and development and felt it was time for a Company magazine, to record events across the Company's domain. Clifton Moore Thomas was the first editor of *The Beaver*. Like many in-house magazines, it dealt with the every-day events of employees' lives: curling scores, social news, promotions, and other events of that nature. Thomas, however, was fascinated by the history of the North.

He made sure each edition included a story about it. Eventually, *The Beaver* expanded and became an independent publication. A second company magazine replaced it as the staff journal. *Moccasin Telegraph* focused on in-house activities in the fur trade and the Northern Stores area in particular. It has since been replaced by the *Nor'Wester*.

Kindersley moved the Company into the world of print, and into Hollywood as well. He signed a contract with a New York agent to produce films. They made 37 of the two-reel black and white movies that were then the rage, as well as one longer film, featuring the history of the Company. This episode soon ended, however, and the Company went back to its more traditional fields as it searched for other sources of revenue.

Charles Vincent Sale replaced Kindersley in 1925. He was responsible for opening one of the largest of the Company's stores. It covered an entire city block in Winnipeg.

The 1930s saw the return of a familiar theme. Once again the Company talked about moving its Canadian headquarters away from Winnipeg. This time, the Head Office thought Toronto would be a better location. The Canadian Committee members, all from Winnipeg, were outraged. The entire group threatened to resign. Headquarters remained in Winnipeg.

In 1931, Sale and three other committee members resigned in opposition to another Head Office proposal. London wanted to form a separate company to operate the retail sales. At this time, Patrick Ashley Cooper was elected Governor, and the proposal was scrapped. The Company remained intact.

TURNING A PROFIT

Sir Patrick Ashley Cooper was from Aberdeen, Scotland, and was a graduate of Cambridge University. He worked with the Bank of England, specializing in companies in financial distress. He was appointed governor of the Hudson's Bay Company in 1931, replacing Charles Vincent Sale, who had been governor since 1925. Through acquisition of certain competitors, including Révillon Frères, Lamson and Hubbard, and the Canalaska Trading Company, HBC was once again able to show a profit.

Chapter Eight
Good Times and Bad Times

The corporate face of the Company was changing. For almost 200 years, its main interest had been the fur trade. Northern trading posts were the traditional meeting places for trappers who brought their pelts to market and buyers who waited for the harvest of furs, ready to cater to the needs of the trappers, with shelves of traps, ammunition and basic supplies, but very few "extras" or non-essential goods.

In its early years, the Company was concerned with keeping people out of its vast trading areas. Canada's far-reaching western and northern lands were largely unknown. In the middle 1800s, settlers began to pour into the southern and central areas of the country. They came from Canada, the United States, Europe and Great Britain. As their numbers grew, settlements expanded, nibbling away at the edges of the frontier. In the settled areas, the fur trade declined and the Company plunged into new ventures. The Company's land sales department catered to the settlers, while saleshops were opened to satisfy the newcomers' needs. One of the finest shops was in Winnipeg. There a three-storey brick building sprawled over a full city block, its bulging shelves carrying almost everything anyone could want. Newspaper advertisements listed jars of lobster, anchovies and Russian caviar, Rose Point lace from Brussels, silk lingerie from Switzerland, and musical instruments of all types, along with more everyday items.

In the North, life continued much as it always had. There was no sudden land boom, no rapid influx of settlers, no instant cities and no need for three-storey saleshops. Native trappers continued to work their trap lines and take their harvest of pelts to the trading posts. There were small changes, such as newer versions of rifles, better ammunition, more efficient traps, and a few new items appeared on the shelves, but even these were basics — heavy shirts or work socks, cast iron frying pans or sturdy cook pots.

Opposite: At a northern HBC store, an Inuit hunter brings in furs from his hunting and considers the purchase of a rifle, 1954.
Richard Harrington, photographer
Hudson's Bay Company Archives / Provincial Archives of Manitoba

Philip A. Chester, Managing Director, Hudson's Bay Company.
M.J. Sym, Photographer
Hudson's Bay Company Archives / Provincial Archives of Manitoba

Suddenly, North America and much of Europe was catapulted into a massive Depression. Stock markets crashed, businesses collapsed and unemployment swept the country with the speed and ferocity of an epidemic. Along with the rest of the business community, the Company suffered. Customers were scarce in the plush new stores in Southern Canada. In time, the economy began to recover, but it was a slow and cautious recovery.

Sales and markets were studied more carefully, business plans were examined more closely. It was then the Company realized it had been attempting the impossible. Over the years, the Northern and Southern departments had followed different paths. Clearly, they now differed in too many ways to flourish under the same management.

The Northern Department was too remote and spanned too vast an area to be run successfully from a distant head office. As part of a Company-wide program of reorganization, the factors in the trading posts were given greater responsibility. On their recommendations, many long-ignored posts were rebuilt and expanded.

In 1925, Philip Alfred Chester was appointed Chief Accountant of the Company in Canada. Five years later he was named Managing Director. Chester pushed forward the trend for change, moving cautiously but surely through the Depression years. Among other initiatives, he expanded the Company's policy of educating its employees by offering courses in merchandising. His vision moved the Company into a modern era.

There was one more change Chester wanted to make. He thought the Company should have its Head Office in Canada, and be run from Canada. This was one step the Company's governor, Patrick Ashley Cooper, refused to take. Head Office had always been in London. Other things might change, but not that.

War intervened before the question could be settled. The Second World War was fought on faraway fronts in Europe and the Pacific, but Canada and other Commonwealth nations added their strength to Britain and the Allies. Many Company employees enlisted. Others served with the Merchant Marine, where the Company's expertise in northern transportation played a key role.

Wartime research spawned many new technologies. One of the most fascinating was radar. For the first time, defenders were able to scan the night skies and see behind the clouds, to detect aircraft that were invisible to the naked eye. A chain of radar stations was established on both the Atlantic and Pacific coasts in 1942, as an early warning system for North America. There was another warning system in effect as well during the war years: the Company played an important but little-known role in Northern defence.

*I*n 1935, Fur Trade Commissioner Ralph Parsons had set up an experimental five-watt short-wave radio station at Pond Inlet and Lake Harbour in the North West Territories, and Wolstenholme, in the province of Quebec. The trial was successful and led to the establishment of a short-wave radio network linking 100 of the Company's more isolated posts. When the Second World War broke out in 1939, this system was already in operation. Company employees cooperated with the military in a number of ways. One important service was providing weather observations. Their data helped guide both commercial and military flights. Another vital function was providing eyes for Ground Observer Stations. In 56 posts across the country, Company staff trained as Aircraft Detection Corps observers.

An even more important network enlisted Indian, Métis and Inuit trappers. While Company staff spent much of their time indoors, the trappers were outdoors and able to observe strange craft in the air or on the sea. In strategic areas, their input could be crucial.

The end of the war brought an end to hostilities with Germany, Japan and Italy, but it was an uneasy peace. Former allies became enemies in a tense situation known as the Cold War, and exclusive control of atomic power slipped from British and American hands. Russia gained nuclear capability, and America suspected other countries were working to develop their own versions of this powerful weapon.

During the Cold War, the United States believed there was a very real danger of attack from the Soviet Union against North America. Toward the end of the Second World War, German rocket scientists had developed unmanned missiles that could carry heavy-duty explosive charges. These V-2 rockets threatened Britain. The United States feared that the Soviet Union had captured some of the scientists who had developed these weapons and, with their help, might now manufacture longer-ranged missiles that could overfly Canada on their way to strategic American targets.

THE *NASCOPIE* AND THE ARCTIC MAIL SERVICE

Whaling ships provided the first mail service to the Arctic but this ended when whaling stations closed at the beginning of the 20th century. Shortly after, the Hudson's Bay Company stations began carrying packet boxes to its posts in the Arctic for residents in those areas.

In 1934, a Post Office representative was sent aboard the *Nascopie* with the government's Eastern Arctic patrol to begin a new mail service. The post office on board the RMS *Nascopie* was equipped to handle all postal transactions from mailing to buying money orders. This service continued on the ship until 1947 when the *Nascopie* was wrecked off the coast of Baffin Island. After that, mail service to the eastern Arctic was provided by the Royal Canadian Air Force.

To protect themselves against this possibility, the North American Air Defence Command (NORAD), built a radar warning system across the Canadian North, a joint Canada-US project providing an improved version of the war-time radar system. This Distant Early Warning line, better known as the DEW line, eventually spanned the continent. Begun by 1954, it went into operation on July 31, 1957. At its peak it linked 31 radar stations, providing high-tech eyes in a sparsely inhabited land. Later, the system was decommissioned in favour of satellite-tracking stations but returned to use during the Reagan years.

There were two other warning lines, the Mid-Canada, which followed the 55th parallel of latitude, and the Pine Tree, which was the most southern. Together, the three lines formed the Ballistic Missile Early Warning System. Many of these radar sites were close to the Company's Northern stores, and brought a tidal wave of activity. NORAD runways allowed large aircraft to land in formerly isolated communities. This likely had a greater impact on Northern development than any other single factor.

The war years brought one other important innovation to the far North and the Arctic and changed the nature of the trading posts, shattering forever the walls of isolation. Radio-telegraphy, which required specialized skills and knowledge, gave way to the easily operated radio-telephone.

HBC aluminum tokens used in Canadian Arctic from 1946 to 1961.
Hudson's Bay Company Archives / PAM

Making use of this technology, the Company established a control station to monitor exchanges between posts and gather information from them. Sales totals were reported by radio and station managers competed for the best results. Radio offered backup assistance in emergencies — medical information was passed along to help cope with sudden illness or injury. It provided diversions as well. The wife of one of the control station managers became famous in her own right. For a time, Mrs. Katherine Isabel Woodrow played piano requests over the radio during the daily broadcasts.

Radio carried messages from the outside world to small isolated communities. Simple greetings from friends and relative, notices from government offices, messages from hospitals and a thousand and one other communications now sped over the airwaves. It was like an expanded party line, or an early version of the Internet. It did not offer the luxury of privacy but did ensure that messages could be passed along more quickly than ever before.

During these years, there was an atmosphere of friendly cooperation throughout the North. Supply ships came in once a year, usually toward the end of summer. During the summer, the traps were put away. Native people moved from the trap lines back into their villages. It was holiday time, when everyone could enjoy traditional Native games as well as the game of soccer they had learned from the traders.

sources for Company stores and houses. Communities purchased and installed their own generators to take advantage of the convenience of electricity. But it would be another decade before refrigeration was installed in the Company stores.

Philip Chester's leadership covered several difficult periods: the years following the First World War, the Great Depression, the Second World War and the post-war recovery. During each of these, he continued planning for future expansions, when conditions would make such moves feasible.

The traditional Native way of life was also changing. Where families once followed the traplines, they now settled in villages so children could attend the new schools. Snowmobiles replaced the traditional dog-teams and sleds. In some cases, men could work their trap lines while still living at home. Overall, they spent much less time in the bush and were far less isolated.

The new settlements and growing population in the North attracted attention from several trading companies. The Baffin Trading Company, formed around 1942, provided competition for the Northern Department for about ten years. Later, village and tribal co-ops were formed, and other independent retailers opened stores.

Above: Twin engine Canso amphibian owned by the HBC, at Spence Bay, 1951. Hudson's Bay Company Archives / Provincial Archives of Manitoba

Once the supply ship arrived, there was no time for games. Men, women and children all helped backpack supplies into the warehouse in those pre-forklift days. The Company provided mug-up (sugared tea) while the work was going on and a party when it ended. Mail was a once-a-year event, arriving at distant outposts along with the annual supplies.

The country and the Company were on the cusp of change. When it came, it came rapidly. Trading posts, once lit by lanterns, now luxuriated in electric lighting. The lights were neither plentiful nor powerful, often just two dim lights in the store and two more in the Company house, but they were a mark of progress. The company's small generators could not produce enough power to run electrical appliances, but it was a beginning. Over the next two decades larger generators were phased in to provide better power

After the war ended, the Canadian government paid greater attention to the North. From bushpilots to charters and small, scheduled airlines, planes provided a quicker way to cross the often trackless terrain. Supplies might still arrive once a year, but mail, high-priority items, and passengers could fly in on a weekly basis or as needed. Emergency medical assistance was only a radio call and a plane ride away.

During these years there were waves of settlement. Energy was the new call of the North, bringing exploration teams and work crews to tap new veins of wealth. The Leduc oil field in Alberta, the natural gas industry of Western Canada, exploration in the Beaufort Sea, and massive development of the Athabaska Tar Sands led to the creation of many instant communities.

Hydro brought another flood of settlers as dams and reservoirs were constructed. Churchill Falls, the Manicouagan River, James Bay, the Nelson, Peace and Kitimat rivers all contributed to Canada's hydro power. Exploration of mineral wealth led to additional settlements — iron in Atikokan (Steep Rock), aluminum smelters in Baie Comeau and Kitimat, copper and gold in the Chibougamau, uranium in Elliott Lake, copper and zinc in Flin Flon, iron ore in Labrador City, copper in Manitouwadge, the nickel mines in Thompson, and gold mines in Yellowknife. Natural resources were tapped on a scale that had never before been possible. The forestry industries exploded on the northern prairies, in Northern Ontario, and in British Columbia.

The Company served these new centres, opening stores and expanding existing services at a dizzying rate. Transportation corridors opened the country further. Major highways, such as the Robert Campbell, Dempster, Klondike, Mackenzie, and the Alaska Highway through Northern British Columbia, gave access to once-isolated areas.

The Northern Stores were now too numerous to be served efficiently from one central office. To meet the changing needs, the Company divided its operation into four administrative units: the East, centred in Montreal; the West, in Edmonton; and the Central division, served from Winnipeg. Winnipeg also served as the headquarters for the Arctic region.

By this time, most Northern Stores were no longer traditional trading posts. The newer stores had little or nothing to do with the fur trade. They were retail stores, designed to serve the needs of a different kind of community. In the mid-1950s, the leadership of the Northern Stores was handed over to Hugh Sutherland.

Among the many changes in the North likely the greatest impact of all came from post-war government policy related to income redistribution and the management of Native affairs. Universal health benefits brought new security to the people. Family allowances, old age security and welfare cheques created a cash flow that was independent of the fur trade, putting cash directly into the hands of Northern's customers. Land claim settlements, such as the James Bay and the Inuvialuit claims, would bring Northern's customers further economic benefits.

The Department of Indian Affairs introduced and financed or promoted major housing developments, schools, nursing stations, hospitals and local road construction.

Bands and hamlets responded with initiatives of their own. They elected councils, assumed responsibility for local government, and played an active role in administration of welfare programs, education and local responsibilities such as road maintenance and garbage collection. In many areas they also provided water and sewer systems and in some districts put in place their own policing systems. The jobs provided by these initiatives added to the employment potential provided by other new businesses, ranging from transportation services to the hospitality industry, retail and craft centres. They offered many new options for northern residents and widened the local economic base.

*A*irports built to support the DEW line, Mid-Canada and Pine Tree lines, now made possible scheduled airline flights. Runways soon serviced other new communities as well.

By this time, most northern communities had converted to electricity, installing powerful generators that made it possible for residents to enjoy modern conveniences. Now, more Northerners than ever before could enjoy electrically powered tools and appliances. They looked to Northern Stores to provide the goods they wanted, including not only television sets but also the goods they saw advertised on those sets.

For many store managers, the changes were almost beyond belief. Two or three decades earlier, goods such as molasses were offered from bulk containers. Spigots tapped into a barrel dispensed molasses into the customer's own container. Like the barrels of molasses, most foods came in bulk and were basic in nature: lard, rice, sugar, flour.

Now customers clamoured for the packaged foods seen in advertisements. Flour and sugar came in small bags rather than huge sacks. Convenience foods such as prepared soups and mayonnaise, cream cheese and cake mixes were added to Northern shopping lists.

Instead of the limited line of basic dry goods once offered (and well into the 1950s Northern was among the very few stores which still sold breeches), store managers now offered a wide selection of clothing for every member of the family.

Topics of discussion in the North also underwent a change as commercial radio and television broadcasts brought news and entertainment to all but the most remote communities. For many years, the CBC was the sole supplier of broadcast coverage in many remote areas. In later years, satellite reception would bring in programs from around the globe, making news of world events instantly accessible to almost everyone.

The Northern Stores, too, explored new methods of communication. Earlier in the century, post clerks and managers learned Morse Code, a dot-and-dash alphabet system that allowed low-powered transmitters to carry messages. As new technologies developed, Northern Stores incorporated them into the Company's communication network.

The North was slower than the rest of Canada to recover from the war years, and for Northern Stores, recovery included many facets. There was the updating of goods and supplies offered in the stores, upgrading of the stores, improvements to housing for employees and education and special services for employees and their dependents.

These were the years when the Company provided vitamin tablets for employees and their families, advice on successful gardening in the North, health and fitness programs that included suggestions on everything from diet to exercise, a library service run by the Personnel Department, and many other projects designed to make life more pleasant for staff and family members.

During this period of refurbishing, restoring and restructuring, the Company realized there was a major gap in its service area. It had no retail representation in the major cities of eastern Canada. The response was typical. They bought Morgan's, a thriving retail chain, that was well established in cities in eastern Canada. A long-time Bay employee, Hugh Sutherland, then general manager of Northern Stores, became president of the Morgan's chain. In a few years, the name was changed and the Morgan's identity disappeared, just as had happened with other stores over the years.

When Sutherland was named president of the Morgan's chain, Des Pitts, another employee who started with the Company as a clerk and rose through the ranks, was named general manager of Northern Stores. As general manager, Pitts continued Hugh Sutherland's and Robert Cheshire's policies of controlled expansion that had made the Northern Stores one of the most profitable parts of the Bay empire. In fact, at one point, profit from the Northern Stores carried the corporation.

During this period, the bulk of the Company's distribution network was centred in Montreal. The Centre had moved twice, from a warehouse at Hudson Bay House to a more up-to-date setting on Perry Street and finally, on February 5, 1969, to Point Claire, where a much larger operation introduced pneumatic tubes and floor conveyors into the system. At that time, it was state-of-the-art technology. But a distribution centre is only the beginning of the process. A critical factor is transportation, moving goods from a central warehouse to individual stores.

Transportation in the North was, and continues to be, difficult and calls for a high degree of ingenuity. Engineers developed the concept of winter roads, built on ice or frozen ground, to handle heavy truck traffic. Even today, in some centres trucks can travel only in the winter, and summer roads do not exist.

Canada's waterways were the traditional method of transportation for the Company in the North. Starting with the original canoes paddled by voyageurs, the Company has relied on a wide range of vessels, from the 32-ton *Nonsuch* through barges and shallow-draft, wood-burning, stern-wheeled steamers such as the *Northland Echo*, *Athabasca River*, *Mackenzie River* and *Distributor*, to the heavy steel steamship *Nascopie*. Some ships were chartered, others purchased outright. In 1990 the container ship MV *Aivik* was added to the Company's fleet.

Aivik was unique. In many places deliveries were made by a supply ship. When the ship arrived goods were loaded by hand onto smaller local ships or barges, and ferried to their destination, then unloaded by hand onto shore and taken to a warehouse.

Aivik's advantage was that it carried its own crane and could sling containers of goods overboard into a lighter, a smaller flat-bottomed boat that could run up on shore where no dock was available.

The first load into the boat was shore equipment, the machinery that would move heavy containers from the lighter into waiting trucks or other vehicles. Then the crane could sling containers of goods into the lighter for transport to shore. When the unloading was finished, the shore equipment would roll back onto the lighter, returning to the cargo ship where the crane would sling it back on board. It was no longer necessary to hand-load goods from the ship to a boat. Cargo was now unloaded more quickly, damages were reduced and there was less chance of accident or injury.

The North West Company divested itself of shipping operations in 1994 when it sold Transport Igloolik Inc. to Transport Nanuk. *Aivik* is one of the two ships Transport Nanuk uses to service the eastern Arctic today.

Railways opened new avenues of delivery and new highways meant some centres could be supplied by truck. These transportation options did more than simply increase the Company's service area. They dramatically reduced the time required for deliveries.

Many residents of the "instant towns" came from southern cities. Even in the Far North they wanted the goods and provisions to which they were accustomed: fresh fruits and vegetables, ice cream and TV dinners, snack foods and specialty items. Distribution centres were enlarged and the range of merchandise widened to accommodate the needs of traditional Northern customers and the new Northerners, both in and outside of Canada. In the late 1970s, Northern introduced the *Selections* catalogue and in the early 1990s offered a *Selections* catalogue, printed in Greenlandic, to residents of Greenland.

New stores opened at locations across Canada and the Company expanded into Alaska as well. At times it was hard to find staff for all the stores. In the early days, most employees were recruited from Scotland and England. In later years, hiring was expanded to include rural and outlying districts of Canada. A few Natives were hired, mainly as helpers.

Gradually education enabled Native Northerners to step into positions once filled from outside. Today, 80 percent of Northern personnel, more than 2,100 managers, clerks and cashiers, are Aboriginal, as are 20 percent of management. Local staff is an important resource. Their heritage of language, culture and tradition allows the North West Company to respond appropriately and sensitively to customers' needs.

Early personnel managers had problems retaining Native staff, who were much sought after. Most employees who took the Company's basic training did very well. But once they began to develop and gain experience, they would be hired away from the Company. Many accepted positions in Native band offices. The Company counts this as an indirect but significant contribution to the development of Native self-government.

One notable exception to the "hiring away" was Len Flett, who became a vice-president. Flett, the fourth generation of his family to work for Northern Stores, opted to stay with the Company and served at various times in Operations, Human Resources, and Marketing. He was the first Native Canadian to join the headquarters staff at Gibraltar House, the head office of the Company, in the role of a corporate director and continues to bring special skills and awareness to the Northern Stores and The North West Company.

Selections *catalogue featuring a full range of clothing, furniture, seasonal items and general merchandise is distributed across Canada and Greenland. Through an agreement with Greenland's largest retailer, Kalaalit Nieverfiat (KNI Greenland Trade) A/S, Selections is translated and distributed to KNI customers, with orders processed and filled from The NWC in Winnipeg.*

SELECTIONS THE CATALOGUE OF THE NORTH 93/94
Northern

Employee training programs have long roots in the Company's history. They began with the original factors and their clerks. During the slower times of the year, the factors instructed their clerks in the finer points of business, everything from how to grade furs and how to order stock, to how to keep account books. Factors and clerks usually shared living quarters, so there were many opportunities for teaching, discussion and instruction. Often these ranged far beyond matters of business and some clerks received a good education in literature, politics, and history along with the more practical instruction.

In later years, when managers brought their families to the posts with them, it was too costly to build separate homes for a manager and one or two clerks. The Company developed a standard form of housing, the 12DB, with four bedrooms, with one of the bedrooms for the clerk.

Clerks have always been expected to study and improve themselves. From the earliest explorers, like Mackenzie and Thompson, to the modern-day clerk, the Company has encouraged individual learning and improvement. A traditional item at trading posts was a basic library, with an annual book allocation for employees at isolated locations. Long winter nights could be spent reading, learning about classic literature, history, geography, mathematics, homemaking, crafts, or simply enjoying light reading. The annual arrival of a box of new books at Post Libraries to augment the permanent collection, was always a welcome event. Northern staff were enthusiastic readers. At that time, it was estimated that each person read an average of 54 books a year.

> **YORK FACTORY**
>
> Fort William was the North West Company's most important depot west of Montreal until the merger with the HBC in 1821. Following the merger, York Factory became the centre for all the Company's trading operations in North America. In 1957, York Factory ceased as a business centre.

Today, public schools provide much of what was once learned on the job and many communities now have their own libraries.

Northern employees have another educational option: Company-designed learning modules tailored to their interests and career paths. The modules involve self-study books and video tapes. The computer network adds another dimension. Modems make e-mail and Internet communication possible, offering direct contact between the student-employee and a human resources department official who can direct questions to the person best qualified to answer them.

Now a new element has been added. Co-op education offers a link between university and college classrooms and retail sales locations, combining formal education with practical experience. Qualified students on a co-op program spend from one semester to a full year at on-the-job experience with the Company before returning to the classroom to finish their degrees or diplomas. An in-house scholarship program can provide financial assistance.

Over the years there have been many changes in the Company. Technology has moved from the quill pen and ledger book to computer programs and spread sheets, but emphasis on employee education has remained a priority.

Chapter Nine

The Return of The North West Company

In the 1960s, the British government unwittingly took a hand in the Company's fate. New tax laws led to drastic changes for firms who did less than 90 percent of their business in Britain. The Company, which did most of its business overseas outside Great Britain, faced an additional tax burden of roughly £800,000 per year. This would decrease shareholders' profits and depress stock values. There was no longer a choice. The head office would move to Canada.

On May 28, 1970, exactly 300 years after the formation of the Company of Adventurers of England Trading into Hudson's Bay, directors of the Hudson's Bay Company gathered at Beaver House in London for the last Board meeting ever to be held in England. That same day, Governor General Roland Michener signed a new Charter for the company at Rideau Hall in Ottawa.

The Hudson's Bay Company was at last a truly Canadian company.

Its resources included 33 large and medium sized department stores, 210 Northern stores, three large fur auction houses, $65 million in stock, oil and gas rights in the Canadian prairies, plus a large transportation fleet. It employed a total of 15,000 persons. It was a far cry from the humble trading post at Waskaganish, on James Bay, so hastily built in 1668 by expedition members from the *Nonsuch*, racing against the onset of winter weather.

Opposite: Today, in both Canada and Alaska, fresh foods and light-weight basic merchandise are shipped mostly by air cargo. Many of the air services are owned and operated by Native peoples groups. Air Creebec serves the James Bay and Hudson's Bay area.
Aircre

Now that the Company was based in Canada, it could more quickly assess market conditions, and react with greater speed. To meet the fierce competition it found in Canada, the Company fell back on its traditional solution: amalgamation or outright purchase. More than a century earlier, when the North West Company posed a major threat to The Bay, the problem was solved by an amalgamation which left The Bay in a controlling position. In the 1930s the Company faced a similar threat from Révillon Frères, of Paris. Révillon was led by enthusiastic entrepreneurs and challenged The Bay, but like the Nor'Westers, they grew too quickly and lacked the financial reserves to carry them through tough times. They, too, were absorbed in a one-sided amalgamation.

In the 1970s, the economy was buoyant. The Company went on a buying spree to strengthen its place in the market. Across mid- and northern Canada, from Port Hardy to Corner Brook, Company stores seemed to pop up overnight, like dandelions in the springtime. Places like Ignace, New Liskeard, Brooks, Camrose, Val d'Or, Rimouski, Carbonear, Douglastown, La Tuque, Lac Megantic, Marystown, St. Anthony, Bathurst, Sydney, Gaspé, Ear Falls, Meadow Lake, Weyburn, Quesnel, Stettler, and Rivière du Loup joined the fold. The Northern Stores expanded into towns and villages across the country until the total reached an amazing 240 stores, employing more than 5,000 persons. With this expansion came a new name: The National Stores Department.

Then an economic slump hit countries throughout the Western World. The sudden downturn left the company financially over-extended.

Between 1982 and 1986 it was forced to divest itself of some of its holdings to strengthen its position in a weak market. Along with other holdings, the National Stores group underwent serious scrutiny. A number were closed outright or transferred to Zellers or The Bay, reducing the total number of National Stores to 178. And to complete the cycle, the name reverted to the Northern Stores Department.

The Northern Stores had always held a unique place in the Company. Now they assumed a separate identity within the corporate structure. One of the indicators of the new status was the formation, in 1985, of an independent buying office for the Northern Stores. It was the beginning of a structural change that would lead to eventual separation.

Soon after this, a group of investors showed interest in the Northern group. There were mixed feelings about this. Northern Stores were the heart of the company. For better or for worse, the Company had made its money and built its reputation in the fur trade. Its traditions and values came from the Northern Department. Sentiment and tradition said it had to be retained.

But for a number of Directors of the Board, economics outweighed sentiment. The Bay decided to focus its energies and its capital in the South, where it did 90 percent of its business. On January 28, 1987, the Board approved the sale of the Northern Stores Department. One Bay official voiced the thoughts of many Company employees when he told an interviewer, "The heritage and adventuring spirit of the Company is gone."

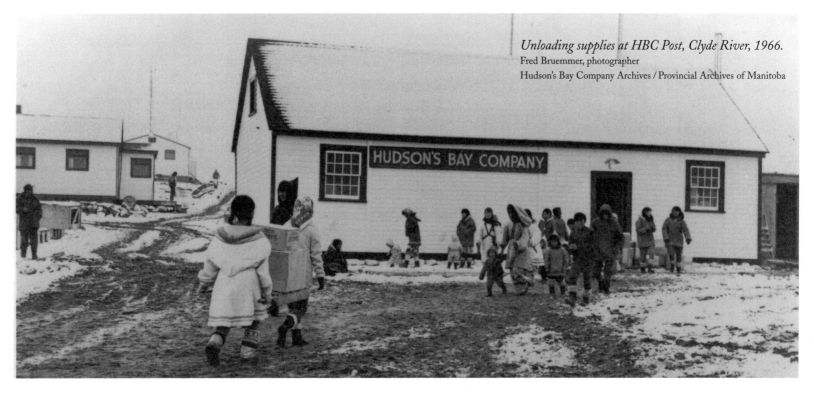

Unloading supplies at HBC Post, Clyde River, 1966.
Fred Bruemmer, photographer
Hudson's Bay Company Archives / Provincial Archives of Manitoba

Like the Nor'Westers 166 years earlier, the Northern Department was thunderstruck when it learned that The Bay was even considering a sale. No one anticipated that Northern's 178 stores would be cut from the vine. But they were.

Marvin Tiller, head of the Northern Stores Department in Winnipeg, met with a delegation made up of Ian Sutherland, Jeff Gidney and Raymond Dore, backed by Mutual Trust of Toronto, Ontario. They were accompanied by the executive vice-president of the Hudson's Bay Company, Iain Ronald, to make a proposal to senior management of the Northern group. Both sides were interested, but the sale would go ahead only if the proposal was supported by Northern's senior management. As it happened, it was supported. Northern believed this was a win-win situation which would once again allow them to control their own destiny. The deal was struck.

Marvin Tiller was named president of the new company. His first challenge was finding a name. A committee began the task of searching for the perfect name — something that would reflect the company's rich, historical past, yet would be appropriate for modern times, and would be easy to remember. One of the most frequent suggestions involved the use of the North West Company name.

Inuit carvings from Canada's North have become popular throughout the world. During the 1950s, the Northern Stores pioneered the marketing of these beautiful sculptures. Today, the Company's Inuit Art marketing division is the leading distributor of Inuit art in the world.
The North West Company

There was something very right about the suggestion. "The North West Company" reflected a long and proud tradition. It differed only slightly from the name of that 1779 Montreal-based fur-trading group: there was no "The" in the original name. The North West Company was adopted as the formal name for the new venture. "Northern" was already a familiar name, that went back to the days when the Northern Stores were a part of The Bay. "Northern" was recommended as the trading name for the company. Both names evolved from the Company's history. From the start, they felt familiar, and they were quickly accepted. The changeover began immediately. It was a smooth transition. Local shoppers soon became accustomed to the new names and business continued very much as usual.

Strategic studies by the new group showed that some stores were surplus and had to be closed. Others simply did not fit the profile of the new company, and these were sold. Company buyers found new producers and new products to add to their list of existing suppliers, but they had lost a valuable asset: the experience of The Bay buyers, and the availability of test-marketing in a wide market. In time, many of the new products and suppliers gave way to more familiar names.

In April, 1989, Marvin Tiller, president and CEO, resigned. Ralph Trott was named president and CEO, and immediately set in place an aggressive strategy of growth and development. Part of that development focused on laying plans to use modern technology to make distribution and delivery more efficient.

In 1992 The North West Company expanded by purchasing the Alaska Commercial Company (ACC). At the time of purchase, ACC had 20 outlets. Eight more were soon added. The NWC had the experience, knowledge and expertise to service this wing of the Northern market. At that time, the Company was exploring the feasibility of working in a circumpolar economic sphere. But a preliminary study of the market situation in Russia's Far East, undertaken in 1994 after the breakup of the former USSR into a federation of independent states, showed that the political and economic stability required for such expansion did not yet exist.

In July 1991, the name Hudson's Bay House in Winnipeg was officially changed to Gibraltar House. Fort Gibraltar had been one of the first permanent buildings at the forks of the Red and Assiniboine rivers. Fort Gibraltar was built in the summer of 1809 and the winter of 1810; it was one of the main NWC posts in the west. At the time, it was the centre of the Company's opposition to the Hudson's Bay post and Lord Selkirk's settlement in Red River.

When Ralph Trott later resigned, the Company once again looked for new leadership, and selected Ian Sutherland. Sutherland was a chartered accountant, who approached the Company in a very different manner than Trott. He was especially aware of the Company's historical background. His father had headed the Northern Stores Division when it was still part of the HBC, and one of his first jobs was with The Bay. He was quick to acknowledge the strength of The Bay's roots in the north, but equally quick to point out that The NWC stores of today had gained new allegiances and forged new bonds.

During Sutherland's term as president and CEO, special attention was given to bringing about Ralph Trott's dream of an improved system of distribution, always a difficult problem in the north and the Arctic. Ever since the days when the early voyageurs faced the twin hazards of distance and weather, the North Westers had struggled against this complex problem. It is almost impossible for retail stores to operate competitively on a totally independent basis, but another set of problems is raised by trying to combine operations and delivery schedules to accommodate a number of stores. There are very real benefits in volume buying and shared transportation costs, but finding workable solutions to providing them had been an administrative nightmare.

For generations, trapping and trading were at the heart of the Company's business in Canada's Northern communities. Trading posts were often the only local source for traps, baits, ammunition, and basic supplies such as flour, salt and tea. However, over time the North has changed, and other economic bases have developed, such as natural resources and power. Aboriginal people no longer rely exclusively on fur trapping. In fact, with reduced world-wide markets for wild furs, trade in this field has dwindled to an historic but minuscule part of the Company's business.

Economic factors are not the only sign of change in the North. It is no longer the isolated area it once was, and the needs and wants of northern residents today parallel those of southern Canadians. These changes have altered almost everything in the North, including Northern's dealings with their customers. Modern-day shoppers are more likely to be interested in VCR rentals than in the latest in traps and baits. Food selections have grown from the minimal supplies to encompass a wide selection of goods, including fresh fruit and vegetables, pre-packaged and frozen goods, and fast food outlets. Drygoods selections have been expanded to include basic and fashion clothing, children's wear, and a wide range of household requirements ranging from furniture to appliances.

ALASKA COMMERCIAL COMPANY (AC COMPANY)

On November 20, 1992, The North West Company purchased the Alaska Commercial Company, based in Anchorage, whose roots can be traced to the original Russian American Company established in 1776 at the time that Russian had claim to Alaska.

When the United States bought Alaska from Russia in 1867, the firm was sold to Lewis Gerstle and Louis Sloss, San Francisco merchants. The new owners incorporated as the Alaska Commercial Company.

J. Derek Riley, Chairman of the Board of the North West Company, returning the HBC flag to the Governor of HBC, Donald S. McGiverin, during the transfer ceremonies of the Northern Stores to The NWC. Riley served as chairman, 1987-1994, and guided the new Company during the initial period of independence from the HBC.

In the centre is Marvin Tiller, President and CEO of the new Company. This official ceremony took place on the Nonsuch, *now located in the Museum of Man and Nature in Winnipeg.*
The North West Company

Northern put into place a catalogue shopping option, which allowed smaller stores to serve customers with larger items they could not normally carry in inventory, or with higher priced goods. Today Northern's clients can use the catalogue or order goods on the Internet, through the Company's web site: www.northwest.ca.

There has been another critical change in the North, which has directly affected the future and direction of the Company. In the early days, Aboriginal peoples were suppliers of furs and consumers of company goods. Over the years, as other sources of income became available, they largely remained in the role of customers. But growing awareness of cultural values, increased levels of education, and an increased interest in commerce soon opened new doors.

At one time, almost all Company employees were European, mainly from England, Scotland and Ireland. In more recent times, employees were drawn in the most part from small, rural communities, or from the Maritimes area. There were Aboriginal people in the Northern workforce, but their roles were limited to unskilled jobs.

New company policy is placing Aboriginal employees, both men and women, in positions of responsibility and helping them prepare themselves for promotions. There are many reasons for these changes. Some relate to company history. As one manager explained, "At one time, the North was terribly romanticized. Employees arrived from the South with a headful of woolly notions and were unable to accept the realities of the North or to integrate into the community. This led to a number of problems."

The Company attempted to address these problems with a hiring policy which tried to eliminate those who did not have the resourcefulness and self-discipline to succeed under sometimes difficult conditions. Meanwhile, members of the local communities provided an almost untapped labour pool. They were comfortable in the North, spoke the languages, knew the customs, and they weren't counting days until they could go "home". The modern-day TNWC policy does not simply accept these applicants, it actively recruits them. Once employees enter the work force, they are encouraged to take part in the company-sponsored pro-active employee training program. It enables them to perform at a high level in their chosen field, and prepares them to progress to managerial and supervisory positions, and beyond.

Employees are enthusiastic about the new programs. More and more, the Company reflects the faces of the communities it serves. Almost all clerks and cashiers, and a growing number of department heads, are from Northern communities. This has another positive outcome. Northern stores have always been supportive of the communities they served, but now this role is enhanced. They have become active partners in community events.

The North West Company's official logo has been designed to reflect the Company's link with the original NWC seal. The beaver gnawing at the base of a tree is still there and is contained within an oval, which is symbolic of the willow frame on which beaver was stretched.

The original motto "Perseverance" has been replaced with "Enterprising". The official Company colour is green, which relates to the vast Northern forests where most of the Company's customers live.

*A*side from Northern's retail activities and the direct benefits of a $40 million annual payroll, the Company finds itself more closely involved in many other aspects of community life. Health and welfare programs are of immediate concern. Educational programs to increase awareness in these fields are incorporated into Northern's community outreach programs. Dieticians are available to work with the community, to discuss the advantages and disadvantages of modern and traditional foods, and to work in co-operation with school programs teaching children the benefits of sound nutrition.

In a long overdue move, the role of Aboriginal people in the North has been acknowledged. Even such a simple matter as signage policy has changed to reflect the many faces of Northern's customers. Where appropriate, store signs carry Inuit and Cree messages, not just English or French.

Cultural programs too are accorded sponsorship, and The North West Company has backed its new programs with solid donations. A set percentage of pre-tax profits is set aside for local events and charitable donations. Over and above that, donations of cash and kind support charitable and not-for-profit Aboriginal organizations meeting a variety of needs in the communities served by Northern stores. Employee participation in local events is encouraged. Additionally, a Northern-sponsored scholarship program offers incentives for qualified Aboriginal students to continue their education, and an environmental awards program helps recognize community concerns.

ABORIGINAL PEOPLE

In 1996, The North West Company created a national Aboriginal Relations Council composed of Aboriginal leaders from across Canada.

Today, The North West Company is the largest employer of Aboriginal people in the north, excluding the government. It employs more than 2100 Aboriginal people.

109

Ian Sutherland, the key player of a private investment group who with the support of senior management of Northern Stores arranged the leveraged buyout of the Northern Stores department from Hudson's Bay Company in January 1987. Sutherland served as president from November 1993 to March 1997 after which he became chairman of the Board of Directors.
The North West Company

By the end of the 1990s, the value of Company assets and the infrastructure to support Northern and Arctic operations exceeded $425 million. As former President Ian Sutherland noted, this is greater than the value of assets transferred to Canada when the Hudson's Bay Company made its historic move from England. As well, Northern is today the largest employer of Aboriginal people in Canada's private sector. Approximately 75 percent of Company stores are in Native communities, and these are staffed by more than 2100 Aboriginal employees. In many communities, Northern is one of the largest local employers. Direct payroll in the North exceeds $45 million annually, and another $36 million is spent each year on freight costs, which benefit northern transportation companies. Wherever possible, Northern's policy is to use companies owned by Aboriginal groups.

Northern's presence has offered another advantage — one that is difficult to evaluate but still important. For many local residents, experience in Northern stores provides an entry point into other careers. In many centres the administration and operation of Band affairs is handled by former Northern employees, often using skills learned through on-the-job training in the stores. This evidence of mobility and opportunity often provides an incentive for younger Band members to stay in school and take advantage of opportunities for higher education in such fields as law, education and commerce.

Another major change between the "old" and "new" North West stores involves ownership. Employees and community residents can and do hold shares in North West stock with some 95 percent of all shares being Canadian owned.

During its short corporate life, The North West Company has achieved ranking among the top ten Manitoba businesses, and stands in the top 200 on the Toronto Stock Exchange. In June, 1993, The North West Company was awarded the "Innovative Retailer of the Year" title by the Retail Council of Canada, and has been recognized as a "caring company" by the Canadian Centre for Philanthropy.

When Ian Sutherland left the Company in 1997, his place was taken by Edward Kennedy, a member of Northern Stores senior management committee. A specialist in corporate development, he served as vice-president of corporate development with The North West Company, as executive vice-president of the Company, and as head of the Alaska Commercial Company before his appointment as Northern's president and CEO.

There have been many changes since the days of the old North West Company, and more since the beginning of the new North West Company. Many are dramatic changes, including the opening of NorthMarts, direct counterparts to stores found in larger southern communities, and Quickstops, which operate popular food franchises, such as Burger King and Kentucky Fried Chicken, under special arrangement with Northern.

Perhaps the most striking is Northern's role as the largest distributor of Inuit art in the world. In the North, tradition is highly respected. Old people and old ways still carry a great weight within the community. One of the oldest and most visible of Aboriginal traditions deals with craftwork and the Aboriginal fondness for utilitarian art, creating beauty by decorating everyday objects. Traces of this talent have survived from pre-historic times. It was the Aboriginal fondness for craft and decoration that made beads one of the most popular trading objects, both in pre-historic times and in the post-contact era. Interest in craft work continues to this day, and it is an interesting aside to history that beads continue to be one of the most popular items on Northern shelves. In continuation of their traditional skills, northern residents still purchase almost 100,000 packages of beads each year.

Just as traditional beads are being woven into new patterns, The North West Company finds itself facing a future that diverges widely from its past. A representative example might be the mail pouch, at one time included in once-a-year supply outfits but today replaced by satellite relays.

There have been major changes in opportunity, in career growth and in economic potential, and the pace of life in Canada's North is unprecedented. Already changes in political boundaries

Members of the important Northern Store Aboriginal staff. The North West Company

are testing the fabric of the country. Nunavut, the newest territory, has been created with elected political representation in Ottawa, rather than appointed leaders.

The North West Company sees its role in Canada's new North as an ever-stronger presence in the market place. The range of services it offers will continue to expand to fit the needs of an increasingly sophisticated clientele. But underlying all the latest trends, the newest styles and the modern conveniences, is a special relationship with the people of the North that goes much deeper than well-stocked shelves in a store.

The North West Company has a long tradition in the Canadian North, and they intend to extend that role far into the future. The North is, after all, one of the last frontiers. And that is where The North West Company has always been at home.

Epilogue

Edward S. Kennedy, President and Chief Executive Officer, The North West Company

Few organizations can compare to The North West Company's compelling, authentic history. At today's North West Company, we consider this to be a challenge. What will be our contribution to the legacy of one of the world's longest continuing enterprises? Time will answer this question just as it has told the remarkable story in this short book.

The Northern store at Berens River, Manitoba

My efforts here are to describe our future at The North West Company and how this future both anticipates and reflects profound change among our stakeholders, starting with our customers. My hope is that you will see the tremendous potential that we see, to grow into an even more vital northern enterprise.

Earlier merchant-traders couldn't have predicted where their adventures would lead. Today we recognize their influence as a major source of change that shaped the people and the land they encountered. Today we can also predict one fact: our future will be marked by an even more unrelenting and accelerating rate of change. The difference is that these new forces for change are swirling around us from all directions and sources. They call us to move quicker, with courage, dramatic moves and enterprising spirit — just like the first Nor'Westers who forged new inland trading routes.

We have answered this call with a plan we call Vision 2000+. It gives us a sharp focus on being the leading provider of food and everyday needs to people in the North. Making it happen means being recognized as our customers' first shopping choice, as a supportive local business, and as the best place to work, while providing superior returns to our investors.

The scope of change we are embarking on fits very well with the publication of our brief history. The first Nor'Westers created an entirely new channel for securing furs, right under the shadow of their larger competitor, The Hudson's Bay Company. Today's North West Company is swiftly transforming itself into a truly dominant food retailer complemented by a highly effective catalogue business. We are changing every one of our stores, reducing our cost of doing business, and building the capability of our people. What better inspiration and guidance for our work than the achievements of McTavish, Mackenzie, and Simpson!

Our Customers

The North West Company is privileged to serve some of the most unique customers in the world. They live in communities that, thanks to communication technology, are virtually right next door and getting closer. But physically, these communities are still very small and very distant: a few hundred or thousand people living hundreds or thousands of kilometres away from the rest of North America. Contrasts can be seen in other ways, from the beauty and harshness of the land to the enduring cultural truths and uprootedness of the society. Change can be a volatile force that both strengthens and weakens these elements

We work on behalf of all of our customers to seek out products and services that enhance their everyday lives. Being their first shopping choice means we know these customers' needs intimately and we have a genuine passion to be the best at meeting them. Opening after hours to provide a snowmobile repair part, special-ordering a case of extra hot barbecue sauce, providing extra large and small clothing sizes in our catalogue, introducing new food items designed for diabetics, and driving down our cost of doing business — these are examples that we are committed to exceeding.

Our customers are increasingly diverse, measured less by language and ethnicity differences and more by age, education and income. For example, it's been eleven years since the Northern Stores Division became an independent company, and nine years since we've changed our name to The North West Company. Yet, we are still "the Bay" to many older customers. This segment represents the heart of what we carefully refer to as our "traditional" market, recognizing that even traditions change. For this group, we

Customers in the produce department of the ACC store in Bethel. Alaska.

are still expected to meet a wide range of basic needs and we plan to do just that, always keeping in mind the unique lifestyle requirements that enable us to be the store that northerners count on.

Our young customers are a completely different and rapidly growing market. Half of the North's population is under 22, contributing to an average age that is ten years below the national average. If there is a typical young customer, his or her perspective is increasingly shaped by the enormous influence of pop-culture trends and style, powered by technology and global brand recognition. The North West Company is a physical link between millions of southern images and the vast physical distance that separates the North from the rest of North America.

To meet the curiosity and expectations of our young customer, we are creating "here and now" convenience with food offerings like Burger King and KFC together with "order and wait (not too long)" catalogue selection for products ranging from fashion clothing to CDs.

In between the young and the older are northern parents and adults. They range from people at the margin, caught in difficult social transition, to those who have emerged as working, educated professionals, actively building a better life for themselves and their community. They all feel the impact of high living costs in the North. In consequence, customers are increasingly sophisticated and tenacious in stretching their dollar. They accomplish this by traditional means like subsistence hunting or in more contemporary ways like buying in bulk quantities or through catalogue shopping. The North West Company's opportunity is to create innovative ways to meet these needs, using our knowledge of northern retailing to serve customers through the most efficient channel: stores, catalogues, or electronically.

Our Communities

Today, The North West Company is a chain of nearly 200 retail stores serving communities with as few as 350 people. At first glance it looks like a mismatch. Aren't these locations a more natural size for smaller, one-store businesses? Why would any company our size bother with such small markets and why would they want to bother with us? Serving the North is still a very complex proposition, which requires specialized and varied knowledge. Our size enables us to leverage this knowledge across Canada and for the benefit of our Alaska operations, whether applied to building stores, recruiting and developing staff, buying at the best price, or deploying information technology. For the community, this means consistency, dependability, accessible credit, selection and quality standards that take the worry out of what would otherwise be a very unpredictable and more costly shopping experience.

There is a second important dimension to serving our communities. It is rooted in our tradition of service and duty to the North. Even today we are almost always the largest of a limited number of local shopping choices. How well we serve a community has an impact that is far greater than most other retailers in the South could ever imagine. We not only readily accept this responsibility, we see it as a link to our heritage and a source of pride and purpose in our work.

Most communities we serve are more autonomous and independent than at any time in the last 50 years. Heightened self-identities and self-determination, coupled with degrees of economic self-sufficiency brought about by land claim settlements, have contributed to building equal partnerships once again in the North. The North West Company has been at the forefront, creating community joint ventures in more than 75% of our new and replacement store projects. We expect and encourage this trend to continue. We are positioned as a trusted and strong partner for Aboriginal entities seeking to develop their local retain or service infrastructures. We see the line blurring between our store and the community both at the local level and regionally, accelerated by the potential of increased investment by northern entities in The North West Company and its asset base.

Vision 2000+ recognizes that a key dimension of our community values is playing a constructive role in community development. There are significant economic gaps between most northern communities and the rest of North America. Our position is to be clearly part of the solution. We seek guidance on this initiative from our recently created national Aboriginal Relations Council. At the local level, we have demonstrated success in several areas, most notably by increasing our Aboriginal management from 12% to 20% over the past three years and by developing comprehensive local training programs.

Education is another essential building block to community development in the North. The North West Company is in a position to be part of many innovative but also practical projects. One example is in Kangiqsujuaq, Nunavik, a community of 450 people located on the south shore of Hudson Strait, approximately 1500 km north of Montreal. Six students run a bakery that offers the community more than 40 different types of bread and pastries. The products are delivered regularly to our Northern store where they are purchased by residents. The results have been increased school attendance, fewer behaviour problems, gross sales of over $20,000, and fresh bakery products now available locally for the first time — overall, a meaningful step forward that earned The North West Company and the local school a 1998 National Community Partnership Award from the Conference Board of Canada.

Our Employees

Frontier Merchants tells us many things about leadership and innovation that connect directly to The North West Company today.

> **NATIONAL ABORIGINAL RELATIONS COUNCIL**
>
> In December 1996, The North West Company created a national Aboriginal Relations Council, composed of Aboriginal leaders from across Canada. Members serving on the Council included the following: Charles Fox, Grand Chief Nishnawbe-Aski Nation; Stanley McKay, Director, TNWC, and former Moderator of the United Church of Canada; Dr. Jessie, Saulteaux Resource Centre; Donald Robertson, Dean, Aboriginal Education and Diversity, Red River Community College; Phil Fontaine, Grand Chief, Assembly of First Nations; Len Flett, Vice President, TNWC, Store Development and Public Affairs and Chair of the National Aboriginal Achievement Foundation; Nellie Cournoyea, Chairperson and CEO, Inuvialuit Regional Corporation and former Leader of The North West Territorial Government.

We learn about truly great men like Simon McTavish, Alexander Mackenzie, and George Simpson. Even more important, we learn about the collective strength of these individuals. They belonged to a team of leaders. Their collaboration and close working partnerships characterized the formation of The North West Company and continues to be the backbone of our effectiveness today and in the future.

How we organize our work and encourage and expect each other to contribute is what sets The North West Company apart. Consider the hivernants who spent their winters in the northwest or the Métis voyageurs who ensured the swift transport of furs and provisions by canoe. They were each experts and leaders, accountable for their role within a wide network of linked activities. At The North West Company, we consider our future to be a tremendous opportunity within the grasp of each of our 4,500 employees — our team of leaders.

Innovation can be defined as the ability to apply new ideas successfully. Sustaining this ability is a scarce resource in retailing today where competitive advantage can be lost in a matter of months. Where we see continuous innovation we also see sustained market leadership, starting with our own history. Every few pages we read about an event or trend sparked by an idea that emerges to propel The North West Company to new heights. Adventurers on expeditions, searching for a new fur trading territory, a passage to the Western Ocean or a new way of life. Challenged by physical hardships and criticized by cautious but influential watchers from the sidelines of London or Montreal. Even by today's standards these were big changes with a healthy degree of risk.

Now fast forward to today's North West Company. We recognize that repositioning an established company like ourselves can be a very difficult initiative. Many organizations fail. Many more do not even attempt it. When we consider our employees, we know we start from a position of tremendous strength. Our culture, knowledge, the purpose of our work and our history have all helped foster exceptional commitment and results. We are asking our people to redirect this commitment to the breakthrough goals and the shared values of Vision 2000+. It is an exciting, even exhilarating opportunity with meaningful rewards, both financial and personal.

Acknowledgements

Besides being a great story, Frontier Merchants is a wonderful bridge from our past to our future. It has been written only because there are people who care about keeping our Company's heritage alive and relevant. For this project, that person was Earl Boon. Earl retired as a Vice-President of The North West Company in 1995. Like all of our retirees, Earl shares an unbreakable bond with past, present, and future Nor'Westers. Earl conceived the idea for this book and then made it happen, with the invaluable assistance of our author, Florida Town, and publisher, Ken Pearson. Earl, thank you for this huge contribution, and for giving us a present-day example of enterprising leadership.

Edward S. Kennedy
President and Chief Executive Officer
The North West Company

Further Reading

Allen, Patricia. *Metepenagiag, New Brunswick's Oldest Village.* Fredericton : Goose Lane Editions, 1994.

Beckles, Willson. *The Life of Lord Strathcona of Mount Royal.* Toronto: Cassell &Company, 1915.

Beckles, Willson. *The Great Company.* Toronto: Copp, Clark, 1899.

Berton, Pierre. *The Last Spike.* Toronto: McClelland and Stewart, 1973.

Berton, Pierre. *My Country.* Toronto: McClelland and Stewart, 1976.

Berton, Pierre. *The Promised Land.* Toronto: McClelland and Stewart, 1984.

Black, Glenn A. *Angel Site.* (2 volumes). Chicago: Lakeside Press, 1967.

Brown, Jennifer S.H. *Strangers in Blood.* 1980.

Campbell, Marjorie Wilkins. *The North West Company.* Toronto: Macmillan, 1957.

Campbell, Marjorie Wilkins. *The Nor'Westers.* Toronto: Macmillan, 1958.

Cowie, Isaac. *The Company of Adventurers.* Toronto: William Briggs Publishing, 1913.

Davidson, Gordon Charles. *The North West Company.* Berkeley: University of California Press, 1918.

Dill, C.L. *Early Peoples of North Dakota State.* Historical Society of North Dakota, 1990.

Dumond, Done E. *The Eskimos and Aleuts.* London: Thames and Hudson, 1977.

Garvins, John W., ed. *Alexander MacKenzie's Voyages.* Toronto, 1927.

Gates, Charles M. ed. *Five Fur Traders of the Northwest.* St. Paul: Minnesota, Historical Society, 1965.

Gilman, Carolyn. *The Grand Portage Story.* St. Paul: Minnesota Historical Society, 1992.

Gray, John Morgan. *Lord Selkirk of Red River.* Toronto: Macmillan Company, 1964.

Hyde, George E. *Indians of the High Plains.* Norman, OK: University of Oklahoma Press, 1959.

Innis, Harold Adam. *The Fur Trade in Canada: An Introduction to Canadian Economic History.* Toronto: University of Toronto Press, 1956.

Jones, T.E.H. *Aboriginal Rock Paintings of the Churchill River.* Regina: Saskatchewan Department of Culture and Youth, 1981.

Kellar, June H. *An Introduction to the Prehistory of Indians.* Indiana

Historical Society, 1993.

Lister, R.H. and Lister F.C. *Those Who Came Before.* Albuquerque: University of New Mexico Press, 1993.

MacKay, Douglas. *The Honourable Company.* Toronto: McClelland & Stewart, 1949.

Mallery, Patrick. *Picture Writing of the American Indians.* New York: Dover Publications, 1972.

Manitoba Culture, *Heritage and Recreation. Through the Ages in Swan River Valley.* 1984.

Manitoba Historic Resources Branch. *Old Copper in Manitoba.* 1986.

Mazonowicz, Douglas. *On the Rocks.* Smithsonian Institution Press, 1980.

McMillan, Alan D. *Native Peoples and Cultures of Canada.* Vancouver and Toronto: Douglas and McIntyre, 1988.

Morrison, Jean, ed. *McGillivray, Simon. North West Company in Rebellion.* Thunder Bay Historical, 1988.

Morton, Arthur S. *Sir George Simpson.* Toronto: J. M. Dent & Sons, 1947.

Newman, Peter C. *Company of Adventurers.* Toronto: Penguin Books, 1985.

Newman, Peter C. *Caesars of the Wilderness.* Toronto: Penguin Books, 1987.

Newman, Peter C. *Merchant Princes.* Toronto: Penguin Books, 1991.

Nute, Grace Lee. *The Voyageur.* St. Paul: Minnesota Historical Society, reprint, 1987.

Pinkerton, Robert E. *The Gentlemen Adventurers.* Toronto: McClelland & Stewart, 1931.

Ray, Arthur J. *Indians in the Fur Trade.* Toronto: University of Toronto Press, 1974.

Ray, Arthur J. *The Canadian Fur Trade in the Industrial Age.* Toronto: University of Toronto Press, 1990.

Rich, E.E. *The Fur Trade and The Northwest to 1857.* Toronto: McClelland and Stewart, 1967.

Silver, Alfred. *Red River Story.* New York: Ballantine Books, 1988.

Stoltman, James B., ed. *Prehistoric Mound Builders of the Mississippi Valley.* Davenport, Iowa: Putnam Museum, 1985.

Van Kirk, Sylvia. *Many Tender Tides, Women in Fur-Trade Society in Western Canada, 1670-1870.* Winnipeg: Watson & Dwyer Publishing, 1980.

Wallace, W. Stewart. *The Pedlars from Quebec and other Papers on the Nor'Westers.* Toronto: The Ryerson Press, 1954.

Index